ASSESSMENT SERIES
K-12 Physical Education

Series Editor
Deborah Tannehill, Ph.D.
Pacific Lutheran University

Assessing Student Outcomes in Sport Education: A Pedagogical Approach

J. Scott Townsend   Derek J. Mohr
Appalachian State University

Richard M. Rairigh   Sean M. Bulger
University of South Carolina   University of Wisconsin-Eau Claire

National Association for Sport and Physical Education
an association of the American Alliance for
Health, Physical Education, Recreation, and Dance

Copyright © 2003

National Association for Sport and Physical Education,
an association of the American Alliance for Health, Physical Education,
Recreation and Dance.

Address orders to: AAHPERD Publications, P.O. Box 385, Oxon Hill, MD 20750-0385, call
1-800-321-0789, or order on line at www.aahperd.org/naspe. Order Stock No. 304-10219

ISBN: 0-88314-748-3

Printed in the United States of America.

CONTENTS

TABLES

FIGURES

Assessment improves student learning, not just monitors it. Assessment is on-going and continuous. Assessments are learning experiences. Assessment provides feedback to learners. Assessment engages students in applying what they learn. Assessment motivates students to achieve. Assessment, if done well, makes teaching "to the test" desirable. Assessment involves tasks that are valued. Assessment values the process of learning. Assessment leaves room for students to monitor and self assess their own learning.

Current reform efforts focused on assessment are about curriculum and instruction as well as assessment. Selecting outcomes that are meaningful and relevant to students is as critical as selecting instructional strategies that will challenge students to strive toward achieving them. Designing assessments that allow students to demonstrate that they have achieved these important outcomes must be relevant and reflect "real" life. These authentic assessments become the link between curriculum and instruction. This suggests that changing the "how" and "what" of assessment so that it is a part of the entire teaching-learning process and provides documentation of student learning is critical; critical to student learning and their desire to learn. We know that carefully considered and well-designed assessments can improve the quality of teaching and increase the amount of student learning. Assessments can track students' performance progress and allow them to take responsibility for their own learning and improvement. Taking ownership will also result in greater motivation and achievement of students.

We have seen new forms of assessment that move responsibility into the hands of learners (self and peer assessment). We have also seen new tools developed to assess student performance in more authentic ways (journals, portfolios, community projects). These assessments are beginning to change the face of curriculum and instruction and the relationship between student outcomes, instructional delivery, and student achievement. Those of you designing and implementing these assessment processes are the source of these changes and the link to future reforms.

The intent of the NASPE Physical Education Assessment Series is to provide resources in the form of a collection of current, appropriate, and realistic assessment tools for physical education professionals. These resources are being developed for physical educators teaching children and youth in schools and for faculty preparing prospective physical education teachers. The series will be a forum for these professionals to share their ideas and successes with innovative assessment strategies.

We intend this series to be an on-going source of ideas, applications, and strategies for assessing student performance. The format will include individually published articles that may be purchased separately or as a continuing series package. Each paper will focus on a specific assessment topic (e.g., journaling, portfolios, game play recording tool), rationale for its use, how it might be used in practice, description of its link to one or more of NASPE's standards projects, and will include an example of the assessment tool. It is our desire that this series become an invaluable tool for teachers.

Deborah Tannehill, Ph.D.

INTRODUCTION

Assessing Student Outcomes in Sport Education: A Pedagogical Approach

The purpose of this document is to describe, in a limited amount of space, the important role that assessment plays in sport education. Given the relative complexity of this topic, the authors assume that the reader is somewhat familiar with both the theoretical underpinnings and practical considerations associated with the use of the sport education model. Readers who are familiar with sport education will recognize how the described assessment strategies contribute directly to the effective design and implementation of a successful sport education season. In an effort to ensure that readers who are unfamiliar with sport education get the most out of this document, we refer them to *Sport Education: Quality PE Through Positive Sport Experiences* (Siedentop, 1994) for a more complete description of this curriculum and instruction model.

The sample assessment strategies included herein reflect the authors' collective experiences working with the sport education model over the past six years. Throughout this time period, our understanding of sport education has continually evolved as a direct result of numerous personal interactions with the undergraduate students, physical education teachers and their students, and fellow teacher educators with whom we have collaborated.

Through these multiple and varied experiences, we found that successful sport education relies heavily on sound assessment and results-oriented professional practice. In essence, assessment represents the foundation of the model. Accordingly, assessment promotes the development of appropriate learning experiences and accountability for student performance and participation. Sound assessment also fosters a culture that helps to hold teachers increasingly accountable for providing effective instruction within the model.

The sample assessment strategies presented in this document have been field tested in a variety of upper-elementary, middle, secondary, and university physical education settings. It is our intention to provide the reader with a cross-sectional representation of the best assessment strategies that we have to date. Ultimately, we hope these strategies spark the reader's interest in sport education and that more physical educators accept the challenge of changing the face of sport instruction for all school-aged children.

## PART 1

What is Sport Education?

Sport education is "a curriculum and instruction model designed to provide authentic, educationally rich sport experiences for girls and boys in the context of school physical education" (Siedentop, 1998, p. 18). The sport education model has the following three primary goals: to educate students to be competent, literate, and enthusiastic sportspersons (Siedentop, 1994). In order to achieve these desirable student outcomes, physical education teachers are required to employ a number of curricular revisions and alternative instructional strategies that are not typically associated with the more widely used multi-activity curricular model.

When using the sport education model, the physical educator (a) lengthens the instructional unit in order to provide the student with increased skill and strategy practice; (b) employs a combination of both teacher-directed and student-centered instructional styles; (c) plans for authentic skill and strategy practice, application, and assessment; and (d) engages the students in the culture of a particular sport by providing opportunities for increased decision making and responsibility (Siedentop, 1994, 1998). Additionally, the sport education model includes six key features that define what it means to participate in an authentic and highly contextualized sport experience. These features are seasons, affiliation, formal competition, culminating events, record keeping, and festivity (Siedentop, 1994).

## PART 2

Why Use Sport Education?

The teaching of team and individual sports is an important component of our elementary, middle, secondary, and university physical education programs. Despite the current trend toward alternative types of programming, such as fitness activities, outdoor adventure, and other lifetime leisure pursuits, the teaching of sport will remain a focus of school-based physical education. The psychomotor, cognitive, and affective skills that a student develops through participation in a developmentally appropriate sport experience provide the foundation for a physically active lifestyle that can be maintained throughout adolescence and adulthood.

Although the potential value of quality sport instruction and participation in relation to the maintenance of a healthy lifestyle is clear, many physical educators struggle with planning, implementing, and assessing teaching-learning environments that effectively engage students with different interests, abilities, and skill levels. Some physical educators, for example, continue to use a multi-activity approach to teach sport. This approach emphasizes exposure to a variety of sports through participation in a series of brief instructional units across the school year. Proponents of the multi-activity approach argue that this varied exposure is important because it provides students with an important basis for making informed decisions about the activities they choose to participate in outside of class.

Several critics, however, have suggested that a number of problems are associated with this approach to the teaching of sport: (a) superficial exposure to the rules, strategies, skills, and culture of a particular sport; (b) isolated sport skill instruction; (c) inadequate opportunities for strategy development; (d) decontextualized game play, and (e) limited student engagement and learning (Graves, Mohr, Wiegand, & Nolan, 2000; Siedentop, 1994; Tannehill, 1998). Unit length, however, may be the most problematic characteristic of the multi-activity approach. Collier (1998) states that within a multi-activity sport unit "it is nearly impossible

for lower-skilled participants to gain the needed practice for skill gains, and game play never reaches its full potential (Collier & Webb, 1998; Hastie, 1996)" (p. 45).

On the other hand, a number of benefits have been reported for physical education teachers and students who are participating in sport education (Alexander, Taggart, & Luckman, 1998; Carlson & Hastie, 1997; Hastie, 1998). The most significant benefits for students include increased investment in physical education, enhanced educational opportunities for potentially marginalized students, and improved levels of learning. This high degree of student engagement can be partially attributed to sound assessment practices.

In response to these positive changes in student interest and engagement, experienced physical educators who try the sport education model often develop a renewed commitment to their own teaching (Siedentop, 1994). The use of daily assessment strategies throughout the sport education season can help not only the students but the teacher to stay focused and motivated regarding the achievement of the intended learning outcomes. Additional benefits for teachers include greater freedom from a direct method of teaching and increased opportunities to use alternative peer instruction and cooperative learning strategies (Hastie, 1998).

In sport education, students are responsible for performing a variety of important roles in the classroom, including being peer coaches, officials, scorekeepers/statisticians, fitness trainers, and so forth (see Appendix, p. 49). By entrusting many of these managerial tasks to students, the teacher creates additional instructional opportunities to focus on individual student needs. When appropriately planned, implemented, and assessed, the sport education season can prove to be an extremely refreshing, intense, fair, challenging, supportive, and exciting educational environment for both the student and teacher.

## PART 3

Planning in Sport Education

Due to the complex and comprehensive nature of the model, physical educators could initially experience some difficulty planning for and implementing sport education in its ideal form. In order to assist teachers in this potentially difficult process, we have developed a systematic approach for planning, implementing, and assessing a sport education season. This pedagogical approach to sport education (PASE) is intended to help teachers plan for, implement, and assess the model efficiently and effectively.

The PASE guidelines for season planning are divided into two distinct components (see Table 1, page 6). The first planning component focuses on six management issues concerning the implementation of the sport education model, such as (a) selecting teams, (b) determining student roles, (c) creating team identity and affiliation, (d) designing team practice and competition schedules, (e) adhering to class procedures and instruction, and (f) grading students.

The second planning component centers on the development of the sport-specific content, which relates most directly to enhancing student learning. These five planning duties include (a) the development of sport-specific skill and strategy content, (b) the design of activity task cards, (c) the design of fitness task cards, (d) the construction of student-coaching plans, and (e) the manufacture of student assessment materials. For a more detailed description of these PASE guidelines, see the November/December 2001 and January 2002 issues of *The Journal of Physical Education, Recreation and Dance* (Mohr, Townsend, & Bulger, 2001, 2002).

PASE Season Planning Guidelines

Planning Component One: Sport Education Model Development	Planning Component Two: Sport-Specific Content Development
■ **Teams Selection** ❏ Determine method of selection ❏ Develop selection materials ■ **Student Roles** ❏ Determine roles & define responsibilities ❏ Link role completion to grading/ accountability system ■ **Team Identity and Affiliation** Provide students opportunities to choose... ❏ Team name ❏ Team colors/uniforms ❏ Team cheer ❏ Team mascot ■ **Team Practice and Competition** ❏ Develop a season block plan ❏ Determine types of competitions/ tournaments ❏ Plan a culminating event ❏ Link practice & competition outcomes to grading/accountability system ■ **Class Procedures and Instruction** ❏ Develop rules & daily routines for the season ❏ Determine when, where, & how each lesson component will take place ❏ Link managerial task system to grading/accountability system ■ **Student Grading/Accountability System** ❏ Determine student learning outcomes ❏ Develop criteria for each learning outcome ❏ Decide how each criteria will be measured ❏ Integrate team & individual points into the grading system ❏ Produce a record-keeping method (i.e., a grade book)	■ **Sport-Specific Content Development** ❏ Select the salient skills for the activity/sport ❏ Identify critical elements & teaching cues for each skill ❏ Design a tactical matrix to determine the salient tactics for the activity/sport ❏ Develop progressive learning activities to develop the skills and associated tactics ■ **Activity Task Cards** ❏ Design task cards from activities identified in sport-specific content development step ❏ Include criteria for progressing through content ❏ Link task completion to grading/ accountability system ■ **Health-Related Fitness** ❏ Develop a set of fitness task cards (at least 3) ❏ Include components of an appropriate warm-up ❏ Account for components of health-related fitness ❏ Sequence activities for safety & injury prevention ■ **Student-Coaching Plans** ❏ Use age-appropriate language ❏ Provide team skill/tactics practice objectives ❏ Include cues, suggestions, & safety considerations for successful practice ❏ Integrate rules & referee protocols ■ **Student Assessment of Learning Outcomes** Design the following assessment instruments... ❏ Skill/Tactical ❏ Application contest ❏ Behavioral/Fair play ❏ Cognitive ❏ Game play/Tournament

Table 1. PASE Season Planning Guidelines

(Referred to on p.5)

## PART 4

Assessment in Sport Education

For the purpose of this document, *assessment* is defined as an all-encompassing process, which includes the intentional acts of using tests to measure and evaluate student performance relative to standards or goals. The general purpose of assessment is to provide meaningful feedback to students, teachers, administrators, parents, and the like. *Tests* are tools, instruments, or protocols designed to measure a student's knowledge, skills, or dispositions. *Measurement* refers to the act of using tests to gather data on a student's knowledge, skills, or dispositions. *Evaluation* describes the practice of determining the worth or value of the data collected during measurement. In combination, tests, measurement, and evaluation form the process of assessment.

Why Assess?

Physical education teachers most frequently use assessment to determine grades for their students. Assessment can be used, however, for many other specific purposes in addition to the determination of student grades (Hasted & Lacy 1998). These additional uses work extremely well within the context of a sport education season (see Table 2, page 11). The ultimate purpose of assessment in sport education is to inform students about their progress towards becoming more competent, literate, and enthusiastic sportspersons. Further-more, well-designed assessment strategies can help to motivate students by holding them accountable for assuming a more highly active role in monitor-ing their own progress and learning. Assessment also provides the basis by which physical educators and school administrators can make informed decisions regarding the relative effectiveness or ineffectiveness of their own curriculum and the employed instructional methods.

What to Assess

Assessment in any educational setting should primarily focus on student achievement of the intended learning outcomes. In school-based physical education programs, the basic learning outcomes are the seven content standards devel-oped by the National Association for Sport and Physical Education (NASPE, 1995). Assessment in any quality physical education program should monitor student progress towards achieving these national standards (see Table 3, page 12). In sport education, the more specific learning outcomes or curricular goals are to "educate students to be *players* in the fullest sense and to help them de-velop as competent, literate, and enthusiastic sportspeople" (Siedentop, 1994, p. 4).

Furthermore, sport education incorporates ten objectives that students achieve through active participation inside- and outside-of-class on a regular basis (see Table 4, page 12). Physical educators who are using sport education are faced with the considerable challenge of aligning their curricular goals and lesson objectives with those of the sport education model and the NASPE content standards. Fortunately, with careful planning it is possible to align and assess both the NASPE content standards and sport education goals and objectives simultaneously (see Table 5, page 13).

An activity task card, for example, addresses the first NASPE content standard by providing a series of developmentally appropriate learning tasks (see Figure 1, page 21). The hierarchically sequenced learning tasks incorporated on the task card enable students to develop competency, and possible proficiency, in the desired movement form. Furthermore, the task card addresses the second NASPE content standard by infusing questions about movement concepts and principles related to motor skill development. The sample task card also attends to the sport education goal of competency, which addresses the development of the skills and knowledge needed to play games satisfactorily.

The sport education objectives that students can demonstrate through the completion of this task card include the following: (1) To develop the skill and fitness specific to a particular sport (i.e., fielding ground and fly balls); (2) to appreciate and be able to execute strategic play in sports (i.e., defending space and coverage); (3) to participate at a level appropriate to their stage of development (i.e., the self-paced and progressive nature of the tasks); (4) to share in the planning and administration of sport experiences (i.e., the self, peer, and coach assessment); and (9) to develop and apply knowledge about umpiring, refereeing, and training (i.e., officiating during learning tasks).

By adopting this comprehensive and outcomes-based approach to assessment, physical education teachers can implement the assessment strategies described in this document and feel confident that they are addressing the learning outcomes specific to sport education as well as our profession's overarching goal of developing physically educated persons. Through this type of assessment, students are also made more aware of the standards, goals, and objectives that they are working to attain in physical education. This enhanced awareness leads to more enjoyable, meaningful, and thoughtful student engagement in their learning related to physical education and activity. Each assessment strategy description in this document includes an explanation of what is being assessed.

When to Assess

Assessment in sport education provides meaningful information in relation to sport education goals and objectives and the NASPE content standards. In order to accomplish the ambitious seasonal goals associated with sport education, assessment needs to be pedagogically focused and well-timed within each daily lesson. If specific assessment strategies are implemented during the appropriate lesson components, then assessment becomes a more authentic and highly integrated part of the instructional process.

The following lesson components are regularly included in a PASE lesson: (a) daily role and duties check, (b) team warm-ups and student-coaches' meeting, (c) team-directed skill/tactics review, (d) teacher-directed skill/tactics instruction, (e) team practice, (f) application contest, (g) lesson closure, and (h) individual/team progress report (Mohr,

Townsend, & Bulger, 2001, 2002). During each of these lesson components, different assessment strategies are routinely employed. During team warm-ups, for example, individual team members complete a sport-specific warm-up and then record related information on a recording sheet (see Figures 9 and 10, page 29 and 30). This information is used to develop individualized fitness goals, to generate a plan for obtaining these goals, and then to monitor progress towards meeting these goals. Each assessment strategy description in this document includes an explanation of when it should be implemented.

How to Implement Assessment

Successful assessment in sport education depends heavily on the physical education teacher's planning. However, the planning process can be overwhelming when a teacher first tries infusing assessment throughout the instructional process. To alleviate this concern, teachers trying sport education for the first time are encouraged to use an experimental-progressive approach to planning for and implementing assessment.

The following guidelines describe this experimental-progressive approach to assessment in sport education: (a) Choose a sport that you know well and are comfortable teaching and assessing; (b) start with a single class; (c) carefully select a few manageable assessment strategies to implement at first; and (d) introduce additional assessment strategies and use more classes as your students become accustomed to the initially selected strategies in the sport education seasons that follow. Several experimental seasons may pass before "full scale" assessment in sport education is in place within every class that you teach. A reflective teacher who carefully selects and systematically implements assessment in sport education in an experimental-progressive fashion increases the likelihood of success for themselves, their students, and the model itself.

Throughout this document many assessment examples are provided that require students to assume various levels of responsibility for assessing their own learning. Teachers should actively prepare their students to use these assessment strategies as a regular part of the instructional process. The following guidelines represent a systematic protocol for training students to take an active role in assessing their own learning: (a) Explain the instrument and its purpose; (b) clarify how the instrument works through demonstration; (c) check for student understanding of how to use the instrument by directly questioning students and allowing for student demonstrations; (d) provide students with multiple guided and independent opportunities to practice using the instrument; (e) offer feedback on that practice; (f) provide more practice in increasingly complex situations that represent how students will ultimately use the instrument; (g) offer more feedback; and (h) hold the students accountable for accurate data collection.

Teachers who use this systematic training protocol are enhancing the meaningfulness of the information that is collected during the season by accounting for objectivity, reliability, and validity throughout the assessment process. Each assessment strategy description in this document includes an explanation of how to implement the assessment strategy.

How to Modify or Design Assessment

Many of the assessment strategies within this document are designed for specific instructional situations, while others are more general in nature and are designed for most any context. However, it is unlikely that teachers will be able to implement any of these strategies without first modifying the instrument, the protocol for using the instrument, and/or the associated learning activities to meet the unique needs of their students and instructional context. When modifying or designing assessment instruments, the related protocol, or the associated learning activities, teachers should account for the following considerations: (a) timing (b) students' developmental level and (c) the instructional environment.

Timing

Timing refers to when and how often assessment is to be used, as well as the amount of time needed to complete the assessment process. In general, assessment in sport education is integrated across an entire season because it is infused throughout each lesson. As teachers plan, it is critical that timing be considered in order to maximize the potential value of the assessment. To accomplish this, the teacher must determine the lesson component during which the instrument will be used, how much time it will take to complete, and the number of times it will be used each season. These critical decisions will be based on the student's ability, knowledge level, and comfort or experience using the assessment instrument.

When using a reflective journal, for example, the teacher can allow students to record journal entries during the team practice or the individual/team progress report component of a lesson (see Figure 15, page 35). If the teacher does not want to use class time for completing journal entries, he/she may assign the journal as an outside-of-class assignment. Whether the teacher decides to have students complete their journaling inside- or outside-of-class, he/she must consider the amount of time it will take for students to finish the assignment. The number and complexity of the questions will greatly influence the time required to complete the journal assignment. Accordingly, the complexity of the questions must accurately reflect the developmental level of the students.

In addition, the teacher needs to determine how often journal entries will be assigned during the season. In order to capitalize on the effectiveness of journaling, it is wise to allow ample time to transpire between each journal assignment. This timing affords students more frequent opportunities to engage in the learning activities upon which they will reflect. The teacher must be careful, however, not to allow too much time to transpire between journal assignments. As the duration between journal assignments increases, so does the time required to complete the journal entry. This journal entry time increases because students are required to reflect upon more experiences for each assignment. Furthermore, as the time between journal assignments increases, students' ability to accurately recall and reflect upon their learning experiences diminishes.

Developmental level

When planning for assessment, the teacher must account for students' developmental levels, which are determined by individual student's age, experience, attitude, and levels of skill and knowledge. The assessment process should reflect the students' developmental level. Younger and less experienced, skilled, and knowledgeable students are generally capable of completing less complex forms of assessment than older and more experienced, skilled, and knowledgeable students. As student age and experience increases, the complexity and requirements associated with each assessment should increase as well.

When using a game performance assessment instrument (GPAI) (Griffin, Mitchell, & Oslin, 1997) to assess skill and tactical performance, for example, the teacher can reduce the number of components and associated criteria to be observed for younger and/or less experienced students. For intermediate and advanced level students, the teacher may decide to include more components and criteria to be observed (see Appendix). However, no more than three components should be assessed at a time. Limiting the number of components to a maximum of three enhances the accuracy of the information being collected. In short, as students gain the experience and knowledge necessary to use the GPAI, or any other assessment instrument, the complexity of the instrument can be adjusted accordingly.

Instructional Environment

Instructional environment refers to the facilities and equipment available in a particular teaching setting. This consideration also includes the number of students in the class. The available space and equipment and the number of students significantly influence the assessment process. All of these variables need to be accounted for when modifying or designing an assessment strategy. When space or equipment is limited and large numbers of students are present, for example, the teacher may choose to use an assessment strategy that requires peer observation (see Figure 8, page 28).

Peer observation simultaneously reduces the demand for space and equipment and engages all students in activities that are related to learning. Peer observations, as well as other forms of assessment, provide alternative, meaningful activities for students who are waiting to play due to environmental limitations. Engaging students in this fashion helps to reduce the potential for off-task, disruptive behavior and increases the opportunity for student learning.

Uses of Assessment in Sport Education

Purpose	Description of Assessment	Sport Education Example
Diagnosis	Determining initial capabilities of individuals before a season of instruction, i.e., pre-testing. Diagnosis identifies individual strengths and weaknesses and impacts subsequent planning and instruction.	• Pre Biography Sheet • Pre Cognitive Test • Pre Skills Combine • Pre GPAI
Classification	Separating individuals into like or mixed groups based upon a predetermined attribute such as skill level, cognitive ability, gender, age, etc.	• Heterogeneous Team Selection
Achievement	Identifying a final level of performance, typically determined at the end of an instructional season, that indicates student obtainment of standards or terminal goals.	• Post Biography Sheet • Post Cognitive Test • Post Skills Combine • Post GPAI
Improvement	Determining the difference in an individual's level of performance between two points in time.	• Pre-Post Cognitive Tests • Pre-Post Skills Combine • Pre-Post GPAI
Motivation	Using varied measurement schedules and multiple tests to monitor student performance, increase accountability, and foster an environment for improvement during an instructional season.	• Pre-Post Skills Combine • Pre-Post Fitness Tests • Daily Reflective Journal • Weekly Statistics
Evaluation of Instructional Units	Determining student achievement in relation to specific objectives for a particular instructional season. Results are used to modify planning and instruction in subsequent seasons.	Assessment of: • Sport Education Goals • Sport Education Objectives
Evaluation of the Curriculum	Ascertaining overall program effectiveness by comparing the cumulative effects of individual seasons to program goals. Results are used to modify curricular offerings and instructional processes.	Assessment of: • NASPE Content Standards • NASPE Benchmarks • State and Local Goals
Teacher Effectiveness	Verifying the effectiveness of instruction through direct observation of the teaching-learning environment or through student performance.	• PASE Teacher Observation Instrument • PASE Student Observation Instrument • Student Achievement and/or Improvement Related to Predetermined Standards
Public Relations and Physical Education	Advocating and justifying the physical education program to educational constituents and the community by documenting and publicizing meaningful outcomes that students are obtaining.	• Posting of Accomplishments • Awards Banquet • PE Web Page • Local Newspaper Articles • PE Newsletters

(Referred to on p.7)

Table 2. Uses of Assessment in Sport Education

NASPE Content Standards

Number	Content Standard
	A physically educated person:
1	Demonstrates competency in many movement forms and proficiency in a few movement forms.
2	Applies movement concepts and principles to the learning and development of motor skills.
3	Exhibits a physically active lifestyle.
4	Achieves and maintains a health-enhancing level of physical fitness.
5	Demonstrates responsible personal and social behavior in physical activity settings.
6	Demonstrates understanding and respect for differences among people in physical activity settings.
7	Understands that physical activity provides opportunities for enjoyment, challenge, self-expression, and social interaction.

Table 3. NASPE Content Standards

(Referred to on p.7)

Sport Education Objectives

Number	Objective
1	Develop skills and fitness specific to particular sports.
2	Appreciate and be able to execute strategic play in sports.
3	Participate at a level appropriate to their stage of development.
4	Share in the planning and administration of sport experiences.
5	Provide responsible leadership.
6	Work effectively within a group toward common goals.
7	Appreciate the rituals and conventions that give particular sports their unique meanings.
8	Develop the capacity to make reasoned decisions about sport issues.
9	Develop and apply knowledge about umpiring, refereeing, and training.
10	Decide voluntarily to become involved in after-school sport.

Table 4. Sport Education Objectives

(Referred to on p.7)

Primary NASPE content standards addressed as a function of sport education goals, objectives, and example assessment instruments.

Sport Education Goals and Assessment Instruments	Sport Education Objectives									
	1	**2**	**3**	**4**	**5**	**6**	**7**	**8**	**9**	**10**
COMPETENCY										
▪ PASE Activity Task Card	1, 2	1, 2	1, 2	2					2	
▪ PASE Application Contest & Scorecard	1	1	1			1				
▪ PASE Cognitive Competency Quizzes										
• Skill and Tactics		2							2	
• Health-Related Fitness									2, 4	
▪ PASE Outside-of-PE Participation Log	3	3		2, 3		3			2, 3	
▪ Game Performance Assessment Instrument	1	1	1			1				
▪ PASE Peer Observation Skill Checklist	1, 2		1, 2	1, 2		1			2	
▪ PASE Fitness Task Cards & Recording Sheet	4		4	2, 4					2, 4	
LITERACY										
▪ PASE Role & Responsibilities Checklist			5, 6	5, 6	5, 6	5, 6	5, 6	5, 6	5, 6	
▪ PASE Etiquette Checklist					5		5	5		
▪ PASE Responsible Sportsperson Pledge				5	5	5	5	5		
▪ PASE Cognitive Literacy Quiz							5	5	5	
ENTHUSIASM										
▪ PASE Reflective Journal				5-7	5-7	5-7	5-7	5-7		
▪ PASE Individual Responsibility Level Rubric & Recording Sheet					5-7	5-7	5-7	5-7		
▪ PASE Event Tasks										
• Event Task 1								5		
• Event Task 2								6		
• Event Task 3								7		
▪ PASE Independent Learning Activity										
• Manager				5-7						5-7
• Trainer				5-7	5-7	5-7		5-7	5-7	5-7
• Reporter							5-7	5-7		5-7

(Referred to on p.7)

Table 5. Primary NASPE content standards addressed as a function of sport education goals, objectives, and example assessment instruments.

## PART 5

Sample Assessment Strategies in Sport Education

In the following three sections assessment in sport education will be discussed in relation to each goal of sport education: to develop a competent, literate, and enthusiastic sports person. Within each section you will find (a) a description of the sport education goal, (b) sample strategies for assessing the goal, (c) the primary NASPE content standards addressed by the strategy, (d) the primary sport education objectives assessed by the strategy, (e) the purpose of the strategy, (f) the time to implement the strategy, and (g) a description of how to implement the strategy.

It is important that readers keep in mind a number of other ideas related to the role of assessment in sport education as well. Assessment in sport education is both alternative and authentic in that it represents "real life." Assessment is integrated in that it cannot be separated from planning and instruction. Assessment is formative in that it occurs throughout the entire season and represents an ongoing process that is intended to document, monitor, and enhance student learning by providing regular, meaningful feedback.

Assessing Competency

A competent sportsperson "has sufficient skills to participate in games satisfactorily, understands and can execute strategies appropriate to the complexity of play, and is a knowledgeable games player" (Siedentop, 1994, p. 4). A teacher can assess competency in sport education by using a variety of instruments and related learning activities with students. The eight instruments and associated learning activities illustrated in this section include: (a) an activity task card, (b) an application contest and associated scorecard, (c) two written quizzes, (d) a participation log, (e) GPAI, (f) a peer observation skill checklist, and (g) a daily fitness activity task card and recording sheet.

Instrument: PASE Activity Task Card – Softball (see Figure 1, page 21)

Primary NASPE Content Standards Addressed: 1 and 2

Primary Sport Education Objectives Addressed: 1, 2, 3, 4, and 9

Purpose: To develop student skill and tactical awareness. The task card also provides the teacher with an effective and efficient means for communicating a series of hierarchical, developmentally appropriate instructional activities.

When to Implement: During team practice

How to Implement: Teachers can post an activity task card in the team home court/field area or distribute individual cards to each member of the team. While under the supervision of the team coach, students can progress through each task as a team or individuals may elect to progress through the tasks at their own rate. Before progressing to subsequent tasks, however, students must be assessed by the appropriate person indicated on the task card. The three levels of assessment that are embedded within the activity task card include self, peer, and coach. These levels are indicated by check boxes - "❑" - in the respective columns. Selected tasks that involve a coach's assessment also require students to record a score. Students can either record information directly on the activity task card if each team member has their own card or on an additional recording sheet.

Instrument: PASE Application Contest and Scorecard – Basketball
(see Figures 2 and 3, pages 22 and 23)

Primary NASPE Content Standards Addressed: 1

Primary Sport Education Objectives Addressed: 1, 2, 3, and 6

Purpose: To develop student skill and tactical awareness by allowing them to authentically assess performance in the context of actual game play. Application contests and scorecards provide the students with valuable information about their performance, related to the specific objectives and goals of a game.

When to Implement: During application contest

How to Implement: Teachers can choose to provide the coach with the application contest description and scorecard during the coaches' meeting or to present the application contest to the entire class. Regardless of the method chosen, if the scoring information is to be useful, it is imperative that the team member recording the scores has a complete understanding of what is being measured and how to accurately record the data. This requires the teacher to clearly describe and demonstrate the application contest for the day. Prior to the demonstration the appropriate person (i.e., statistician) receives the scorecard and fills out the biographical information. During the demonstration the statistician can practice recording data.

Only the shaded areas on the scorecard are used during the application contest. This shading helps to focus the statistician's attention on only the relevant parts of the scorecard for a particular day. The shaded areas change according to the type of information that the teacher wants the statistician to collect. As the season progresses and statisticians become more skilled, the type and amount of information collected becomes more complex. By the end of the season statisticians should be able to collect all of the information called for by the scorecard. Leading up to this time, however, the teacher and team coach should regularly check the statistician's records to ensure the accuracy of the information being collected.

Instrument: PASE Cognitive Competency Quiz (Skill/Tactics and Health-Related Physical Fitness) – Tennis
(see Figures 4 and 5, pages 24 and 25)

Primary NASPE Content Standards Addressed: 2 and 4

Primary Sport Education Objectives Addressed: 2 and 9

Purpose: To allow students to demonstrate the degree of knowledge they posses in relation to the skills, tactics, and related concepts being taught.

When to Implement: During team-directed skill tactics review or team practice

How to Implement: Teachers can choose to either administer this quiz to the entire team or to each individual member of the class. The quiz is designed to assess students' knowledge on a variety of different levels. These levels range from rote memorization, to comprehension, to application, to analysis, to synthesis, to evaluation. According to the number and nature of the questions and student's developmental levels, the teacher must provide the students with a sufficient amount of time to complete the quiz. The teacher can provide all of the students with a set amount of time or allow for individual differences in test taking speed. Students can record their answers directly on the test or on an additional sheet.

Instrument: PASE Outside-of-Class Physical Activity Participation Log
(see Figure 6, page 26)

Primary NASPE Content Standards Addressed: 2 and 3

Primary Sport Education Objectives Addressed: 1, 2, 4, 6, and 9

Purpose: To encourage regular participation in physical activity on most, if not all days of the week, by affording students the opportunity to plan and engage in personally meaningful learning experiences outside-of-class. This assessment provides the teacher with a valuable indicator of the extent to which students are engaging in health-enhancing physical activity during their own leisure time.

When to Implement: Outside-of-physical education class

How to Implement: At the end of each week, the teacher provides the individual students or teams with copies of the participation log. The students are instructed to use the weekend to plan for the upcoming week's physical activity participation schedule. Teachers should encourage the students to practice the skills and tactics being taught in the current sport season, but should not limit student choice. Students select a minimum of four days in which to plan for physical activity participation outside-of-class.

At the weeks end or after engaging in the planned physical activity experience, students should record the activity they actually performed, how long they were active, and who they chose to participate with. Each student is also asked to rate how much they enjoyed the physical activity using the Rating of Perceived Enjoyment (RPE) scale. This learning activity allows the students to track their ability to set and achieve goals related to their own physical activity preferences.

Instrument: GPAI – Ultimate
(see Figure 7, page 27)

Primary NASPE Content Standards Addressed: 1

Primary Sport Education Objectives Addressed: 1, 2, 3, and 6

Purpose: To determine the extent to which a student can solve tactical problems by executing skills, making decisions, and moving during game play. The GPAI provides information about the players when they have and do not have the disc.

When to Implement: During application contest

How to Implement: Teachers may choose to complete this assessment on their own or teach students to gather game play data. The teacher must first decide which components of game performance should be included in respect to the sport being practiced (see GPAI in Appendix). Specific criteria are then established to further define the components being measured. In Figure 7 on page 27, for example, the one component being measured is skill execution. The skills evaluated during Ultimate game play include controlling a received pass and throwing a disc that is level and successfully reaches its intended target. If this behavior is observed as described, the action is deemed efficient and a mark is placed in the appropriate column. Should the same player attempt a throw that is not level and/or falls short of the intended target, a mark would be placed in the inefficient column underneath skill execution.

Following the completion of the game or time allotted for data collection, the statistician summarizes the data by using the index calculation formulas located at the bottom of the page. These results of the index calculations provide the teacher and learner with a ratio of appropriate to inappropriate or efficient to inefficient actions for game players. While the index being used may change depending on the context, the formula is always a ratio of appropriate to inappropriate or efficient to inefficient actions. This information can then be used for instructional planning and individual student goal-setting. Students can also create their own GPAI or use a template like the one provided in the Appendix.

Instrument: PASE Peer Observation Skill Checklist – Throwing *(see Figure 8, page 28)*

Primary NASPE Content Standards Addressed: 1 and 2

Primary Sport Education Objectives Addressed: 1, 3, 4, 6, and 9

Purpose: To develop student skill and analytic ability, while affording the teacher an effective means for communicating information to student peer groups. Peer observation skills checklists present students with an opportunity to receive immediate feedback from a teammate and to develop the ability to analyze the skill of another performer.

When to Implement: During team-directed skill/tactics review, or team practice

How to Implement: The teacher provides a checklist per team member. Students, after having been provided sufficient time to practice the skill of interest, will begin to perform and analyze one another's performance. While one partner is performing the other is observing one instructional cue at a time. The partner is observing the skill performance to determine whether or not the performer demonstrates the instructional cue correctly. Observing one instructional cue at a time, the observer/analyzer places a check mark in the yes or no box depending on the relative success of the performer.

Although the observer/analyzer is attending to only one instructional cue per trial, the performer should demonstrate the entire skill on each trial. Following each trial, the observer/analyzer provides feedback to the performer about their performance on the instructional cue of interest. In addition, the performer needs to complete multiple trials for each instructional cue. Multiple trials will enhance the accuracy of the data collected per instructional cue and will give the performer multiple opportunities to improve their performance on that particular instructional cue.

For the skill of throwing, as depicted in Figure 8, there are four critical features. Accordingly, the performer throws five times for each instructional cue for a total of 20 trials. Following the completion of the 20th trial, the observer/analyzer totals up the amount of correctly performed instructional cues and uses the rating scale to categorize the thrower's performance. A set of questions are then used to focus the thrower on goal setting to improve upon their future performance.

Instrument: PASE Fitness Task Cards and Recording Sheet – Volleyball
(see Figures 9 and 10, pages 29 and 30)

Primary NASPE Content Standards Addressed: 2 and 4

Primary Sport Education Objectives Addressed: 1, 3, 4, and 9

Purpose: To develop student health- and skill-related physical fitness levels and knowledge of appropriate activities that comprise a total body warm-up. Additionally, it affords the teacher a means of communicating and holding students accountable for performing a sequence of developmentally appropriate activities that could be used to prepare for sport-specific activity. This assessment strategy also provides an efficient method for tracking student health- and skill-related physical fitness scores over time.

When to Implement: During team warm-ups

How to Implement: Teachers can post the fitness task card and recording sheet at each team home court area or they may supply them to the team fitness trainer for distribution. It is recommended that the team fitness trainer select the task card that the team will perform for that lesson's particular warm-up. The fitness trainer supervises the warm-up and monitors his/her team's progress. It is suggested that each team member move at an individual pace through the fitness activities and record their progress on their own personal recording sheets. The student simply circles the fitness task card selected (A, B, or C) and then checks off each task completed to criteria. In addition to completing the tasks, each member should also respond to the effort level indicators included on the recording sheet.

Assessing Literacy

A literate sportsperson "understands and values the rules, rituals, and traditions of sports and distinguishes between good and bad sports practices, whether in children's or professional sport. A literate sportsperson is both a more able participant and more discerning consumer, whether fan or spectator" (Siedentop, 1994, p.4). Student literacy in sport education can be assessed in a wide variety of ways. The sample assessment instruments described in this section include: (a) a role and responsibility checklist, (b) an etiquette checklist, (c) the responsible sportsperson pledge, and (d) a written quiz.

Instrument: PASE Role and Responsibilities Checklist – Dance
(see Figure 11, page 31)

Primary NASPE Content Standards Addressed: 5 and 6

Primary Sport Education Objectives Addressed: 3, 4, 5, 6, 7, 8, and 9

Purpose: To afford students the opportunity to identify and successfully perform additional roles within a sporting culture beyond that of player and team member. Furthermore, it provides increased responsibility for students in the planning, implementation, and assessment of a sport education season. This increased ownership is important in developing physically educated students who appreciate the culture of a sport in its entirety.

When to Implement: During role and responsibilities check and progress reporting

How to Implement: The teacher provides this checklist to each student by keeping it in a folder at each team home court/field area (Graves & Townsend, 2000). After entering the gymnasium, the students identify their role for the class session and the associated criteria for performing successfully. At this point, the checklist is used to inform students of the expectations for their performance during the class. The students also use this instrument during the completion of their progress reports following the lesson closure. At that point, the student identifies whether or not each role responsibility was performed successfully. The teacher can cross-reference their own notes of student performance with these self-assessment checklists to ensure a degree of quality control and appropriate decision-making on the part of the students.

Instrument: PASE Etiquette Checklist – Golf *(see Figure 12, page 32)*

Primary NASPE Content Standards Addressed: 5

Primary Sport Education Objectives Addressed: 5, 7, and 8

Purpose: To develop student knowledge and

awareness of the etiquette issues associated with a specific sport. The checklist provides a systematic method for tracking the development of behaviors that are not necessarily skill-related, but add to the total quality of the sport experience.

When to Implement: During team practice and/or application contest

How to Implement: The teacher provides the students with the etiquette checklist during team practice or the application contest. Each student uses the checklist to determine the proper etiquette that should be demonstrated during a round of golf, for example. In order to arrange the teaching-learning environment to encourage proper etiquette, players should not mark successful completion of each indicator until they have left the green and proceeded to the next tee area. At this time, the checklist can be completed for the last hole played.

A checkmark system is used to mark successful completion of each indicator. Partners should inspect each other's checklist every few holes to ensure the accuracy of the information being collected. At the completion of the round, both players sign at the bottom to attest to the accuracy of the data recorded. After completion of the golf game, the student adds up the number of etiquette indicators that were not performed during the round and uses the scoring rubric to identify their own level of etiquette. The corresponding questions are designed to foster critical reflection and goal setting behaviors.

Instrument: PASE Responsible Sportsperson Pledge (see Figure 13, page 33)

Primary NASPE Content Standards Addressed: 5

Primary Sport Education Objectives Addressed: 4, 5, 6, 7, and 8

Purpose: To develop student awareness of fair play expectations related to responsible sport participation. By reading, copying, and signing the pledge, each student demonstrates a basic level of awareness concerning responsible sportsmanship. This assessment strategy also serves as a behavioral contract between student and teacher. As such, the pledge provides the teacher with a set of behaviors about which he/she can provide specific feedback during the season.

When to Implement: During initial lessons of sport education season

How to Implement: The expectations for the sport season should be clearly discussed early on so each student is aware of the behaviors that are appropriate and inappropriate. The teacher provides each team with a written contract to be read, copied, and signed by each team member. Having students copy a statement and sign a pledge to act appropriately adds an additional level of personal accountability. It also effectively communicates to students the fact that inappropriate choices lead to negative consequences. In a situation where students are making inappropriate choices, a reminder of their pledge to be a responsible sportsperson can serve as a prompt to refocus their decision-making.

Instrument: PASE Cognitive Literacy Quiz (Roles, Rules, and Rituals) – Flag Football (see Figure 14, page 34)

Primary NASPE Content Standards Addressed: 5

Primary Sport Education Objectives Addressed: 7, 8, and 9

Purpose: To allow students to demonstrate the degree of knowledge they possess in relation to the rules, roles, and rituals of the sport being taught.

When to Implement: During team-directed skill tactics review or team practice

How to Implement: Teachers can choose to administer this quiz to the entire team or to each individual member of the class. The quiz is designed to investigate student knowledge of a variety of concepts at different levels of complexity. Students can either record information directly on the quiz if each team member has their own or on an additional sheet.

Assessing Enthusiasm

An enthusiastic sportsperson "participates and behaves in ways that preserve, protect, and enhance the sports culture, whether it is a local youth sport culture or a national sport culture" (Siedentop, 1994, p.4). To assess enthusiasm in sport education a teacher can use an assortment of instruments and associated learning activities. To demonstrate how a teacher can assess enthusiasm four instruments and related learning activities are described in this section: (a) a journaling activity, (b) an individual responsibility rubric and recording sheet, (c) three events tasks, and (d) three independent learning activities.

Instrument: PASE Reflective Journal
(see Figure 15, page 35)

Primary NASPE Content Standards Addressed: 5, 6, and 7

Primary Sport Education Objectives Addressed: 4, 5, 6, 7, and 8

Purpose: To provide students with opportunities for self-expression and self-analysis of their behavior and the personal meaning of physical activity. The journal provides a vehicle for the processing of both internal and external information about the individual's performance and perceptions about that performance.

When to Implement: Outside of physical education class

How to Implement: The teacher provides the journaling questions during the closure of a particular lesson. Each student should be provided the set of questions. This instrument could be given at the week's end and assigned as homework for the following class period. Depending on your physical education schedule, the teacher could assign these questions during weeks 1, 3, and 5. If your program does not offer daily physical education, a better schedule may be following lessons 7, 14, and 21. The journal entries are not viewed as right or wrong since they represent personal performance and perception. The criterion for the quality of the answers, however, is used to ensure complete responses and encourage critical self-reflection.

Instrument: PASE Individual Responsibility Level Rubric and Recording Sheet *(see Figures 16 and 17, pages 36 and 37)*

Primary NASPE Content Standards Addressed: 5, 6, and 7

Primary Sport Education Objectives Addressed: 5, 6, 7, and 8

Purpose: To provide students with an increased awareness of their level of decision-making during the sport education season. The related scoring rubric provides students with a framework for determining the appropriateness of their behavior and allows for identification of areas where more effective decision-making is needed. The scoring rubric and associated recording sheet encourages increased accountability on the part of the students for the positive and negative choices made throughout a particular lesson.

When to Implement: During progress reporting

How to Implement: At the lesson end, students refer to their personal recording sheet. The students, using the scoring rubric as a guide, identify the level of responsibility at which they participated during the lesson. The rubric is divided into categories of preparedness, transitioning, on-task behavior, sportsmanship, and assessment. Collectively, these categories account for the major decisions that students make during a PASE lesson. After they select the level that best represents their performance, the individual responsibility level is then recorded along with a brief rationale. The student then sets a responsibility level goal for the next lesson. Along with the goal, it is also important for the student to indicate a strategy for reaching that goal.

Instrument: PASE Event Tasks (1, 2, and 3)
(see Figure 18, page 38)

Primary NASPE Content Standards Addressed: 5, 6, and 7

Primary Sport Education Objectives Addressed: 8

Purpose: To provide students with a performance task that enables them to apply critical thinking skills to a real world scenario. This instrument produces information that can be used to investigate student problem solving skills, social responsibility, acceptance of ideas, teamwork, and authentic application of sport issues.

When to Implement: During team practice

How to Implement: The teacher provides each team with a case scenario that they need to complete as a group. An allotment of 30 to 50 minutes is adequate depending on the complexity of the scenario and the class time constraints. The activity is designed to encourage teamwork and cooperation during the problem-solving process. In order to foster this environment, the teacher should discuss the scoring rubric prior to student engagement in the task development.

Due to the open-ended nature of the task, the scoring rubric is not used to grade correct and incorrect responses. The students are scored on their ability (a) to provide comprehensive rationales for the decisions they make, (b) to include ideas from all team members, (c) to assign different responsibilities to each team member during the design of the event task, and (d) to resolve conflicts in an appropriate and productive manner.

Instrument: PASE Independent Learning Activity (All Roles) *(see Figure 19, page 39)*

Primary NASPE Content Standards Addressed: 5, 6, and 7

Primary Sport Education Objectives Addressed: 4, 5, 6, 7, 8, 9, and 10

Purpose: To provide students with an opportunity to practice the roles that they have learned about during the sport season in an outside-of-class setting. This type of learning experience may also encourage further student participation in volunteer activities in the larger community.

When to Implement: Outside-of-physical education class

How to Implement: The teacher provides the students with the assignment during the second half of the season, after the various roles have been practiced in the physical education class-room and the students have demonstrated role competence. The teacher should provide the students with a choice of roles so that they can select one that matches well with their perceived strengths and personal interests.

Once a student has selected a role and become more familiar with the associated responsibilities, he/she should identify the different practice opportunities that exist in the community. The teacher is responsible for assisting students in finding placements that will allow them to adequately engage in their selected role. Due to the highly variable nature of the roles and contexts in which the associated responsibilities will be performed, the use of a scoring rubric, which relates to the student's decision-making process and preparation for the assignment is appropriate for assessing this activity.

PASE ACTIVITY TASK CARD – SOFTBALL

Skill(s): • Fielding Ground Balls   **Tactic(s):** • Defending Bases/Coverage
• Fielding Fly Balls

Learning Tasks	Self	Peer	Coach
1. Under the coach's direction, practice the umpire signals for a runner who is safe and for a runner who is out 10 times each.			❏
2. In groups of four, practice fielding ground and fly balls. Partner A will begin the play by throwing a ground ball or a fly ball, within the boundaries, to partner B. Partner B will then field the ball & attempt a force-out throw to partner C. After player A has initiated the play, he/she attempts to run and safely cross the base. Partner D role-plays as the umpire and uses the appropriate signal to indicate if the base runner was safe or out. Repeat sequence two times and then rotate positions.		❏	
3. Alone, without the ball, take the appropriate infielder's stance 10 times.	❏		
4. Throw a ball at a low level to a wall 15 yds. away and field the rebound for 2 min.	❏		
5. Throw a ball at a medium level to a wall 20 yds. away and field the rebound for 2 min.	❏		
6. How many balls can you throw at a low-medium level and field from the wall in 30 sec.? Record.	#___		❏
7. With a partner 20 yds. away, field ground balls without having to move for 2 min.		❏	
8. With a partner 20 yds. away, field ground balls moving to the right and left for 1 min.		❏	
9. With a partner 20 yds. away, field ground balls and immediately make a force-out throw for 1 min.		❏	
10. How many ground balls can you field and return with a force-out throw in 30 sec.? Record.	#___		❏
11. Alone, without a ball, take the appropriate outfielder's stance 10 times.	❏		
12. Alone, toss a ball straight up, approx. 20 ft into the air, and catch the fly ball for 1 min.	❏		
13. With a partner 15 yds. away, field fly balls without having to move for 2 min.		❏	
14. With a partner 20 yds. away, field fly balls moving forward and backwards for 1 min.		❏	
15. With a partner 20 yds. away, field fly balls and immediately make a force-out throw for 1 min.		❏	
16. How many fly balls can you field and return with a force-out throw in 45 sec.? Record.	#___		❏
17. With a partner 20 yds. away, randomly throw ground and fly balls and attempt to field the balls and make a force-out throw for 2 min.	❏		
18. Without knowing which type ball is being delivered, how many balls can you field and throw in 45 sec.?	#___		❏
19. In groups of four, practice fielding ground and fly balls. Partner A will begin the play by throwing a ground ball or a fly ball, within the boundaries, to partner B. Partner B will then field the ball & attempt a force-out throw to partner C. After player A has initiated the play, he attempts to run and safely cross the base. Partner D role-plays as the umpire and uses the appropriate signal to indicate if the base runner was safe or out. Rotate positions after each sequence. A. Is it easier to make a force play from a ground ball or fly ball? Why? B. What are three ways to increase the chances of forcing the runner out? C. How can the umpire increase the likelihood that she will make the correct call?			❏
20. Repeat #19. This time partner A earns 1 point for a safe base scored. The fielder receives 1 point if he can successfully field the ball. Partner C earns 1 point if she successfully catches the ball at the base, and the umpire earns 1 point if he uses the correct signals. Record scores. Repeat until everyone has earned five points.			❏

(Referred to on p.7 & p.14)

Figure 1. PASE Activity Task Card – Softball – Focus: Force Plays, Lesson 5

PASE APPLICATION CONTEST - BASKETBALL

Season: Basketball	**Official's Signals and Violations:**	• **Traveling and Carrying** • **Double Dribbling** • **Illegal Use of Hands**

Objectives:

- Perform short-range jump shots
- Dribble to reposition and use V- and L-cuts to create passing lanes
- Use appropriate defensive pressure

Team Goals:

- Score the maximum number of points in a 3 vs. 3 modified game

Application Description:

- 3 vs. 3
- Play two 5-minute halves
- Half court
- Game begins with a jump ball by the official
- Ball must be cleared beyond the 3-point arc on every change of possession
- Two free throws awarded for each foul

Scorekeeper's Guidelines:

- Record 2 points for successfully completed jump shots inside the 3-point arc
- Record 0 points for shots taken beyond the 3-point arc
- Record 1 point for successfully completed foul shots
- Record 1 point for each steal
- Record each team member's individual score
- Combine all team members' points for a total team score

Referee's Guidelines:

- Award no points if the same player shoots and scores on two consecutive jump shots
- Use the proper signals for scoring
- Use the proper clock-related signals
- Use the proper violation signals

(Referred to on p.15)

Figure 2. PASE Application Contest – Basketball – Focus: Motion Offense, Lesson 10

PASE APPLICATION CONTEST SCORECARD - BASKETBALL

Directions: Shaded areas must be filled in by scorekeeper

☐ Home ☐ Away

Team	Coach	Date		FINAL SCORE
Scorekeeper	Opponent			

Scoring by Half

	1st – 5 min.	2nd – 5 min.	OT

Individual Scoring / Summary

Player	Fouls	1st	2nd	OT	2 FG A	2 FG M	3 FG A	3 FG M	FT A	FT M	Steals	Reb.	PTS
John Smith	1 2 3 4 5	II	III		2	1			2	2	1		5
	1 2 3 4 5												
	1 2 3 4 5												
	1 2 3 4 5												
	1 2 3 4 5												
	1 2 3 4 5												
	1 2 3 4 5												
	1 2 3 4 5												
Totals													

Team Fouls

1	2	3	4	5	6	7	8	9	10

Alternating Possession/Jump Ball →

Team Time-Outs

	1		2		3		4		5	
Home		Away	Home	Away	Home	Away	Home	Away	Home	Away

Running Score

Home	Away	Home	Away	Home	Away	Home	Away	Home	Away	Home	Away	Home	Away	Home	Away	Home	Away	Home	Away	Home	Away	Home	Away	Home
1	2	3	4	5	6	7	8	9	10	11	12	13	14	15	16	17	18	19	20	21	22	23	24	25
26	27	28	29	30	31	32	33	34	35	36	37	38	39	40	41	42	43	44	45	46	47	48	49	50
51	52	53	54	55	56	57	58	59	60	61	62	63	64	65	66	67	68	69	70	71	72	73	74	75
76	77	78	79	80	81	82	83	84	85	86	87	88	89	90	91	92	93	94	95	96	97	98	99	100

✎ Coach's Signature _____

✎ Scorekeeper's Signature _____

(Referred to on p.15)

Figure 3. PASE Application Contest Scorecard – Basketball – Focus: Motion Offense, Lesson 10

PASE COGNITIVE COMPETENCY QUIZ – TENNIS

| Skills: | • Forehand Ground Stroke | Tactic: | • Creating space using ground strokes |
| | • Backhand Ground Stroke | | |

Directions: Answer the following questions in the space provided.

Question Type	Question	Answers
1. Multiple Choice	A forehand ground stroke, when hit from the back foot, will tend to go	A. To the right of the intended target B. To the left of the intended target C. Straight across the net D. Into the net
2. True or False	It is an advantage to use the Eastern backhand grip over any other backhand grip because it provides the best support for the racket at ball contact.	True or False
3. Fill in the Blank	_____ is an effective tactic used to create open space in the opponent's court.	A. A powerful forehand B. Attacking a drop shot C. Recovery to center court D. Side to side ground strokes
4. Matching	Match the following definition with the correct skill terminology: A. A way of holding the racket so that the player does not have to change grips between the forehand and the backhand grip. B. A stroke that a right-handed player hits by reaching across the body to the left side. C. A stroke that a right-handed player hits on the right side of his/her body. D. A grip in which the V formed by the thumb and index finger is above and slightly toward the right of the racket handle as a right-handed player prepares to hit a forehand.	Forehand stroke _____ Continental grip _____ Eastern grip _____ Backhand stroke _____

5. Short Answer

① ② ③

You are in a rally with an opponent using both forehand and backhand ground-strokes. If your first three shots landed in the same general area (as shown in the diagram to the left), where is the best place to hit the next shot? Label the diagram using the symbol ④ to mark where you would hit the fourth shot and explain why.

_____

_____

_____

_____

Answer Key: (1) B   (2) True   (3) D   (4) C, A, D, B   (5) Deep or short and to the right, to create space in the attack

(Referred to on p.15)

Figure 4. PASE Cognitive Competency Quiz – Tennis – Focus: Tennis Ground Strokes, Quiz 1

Name: _____

PASE COGNITIVE COMPETENCY QUIZ – TENNIS		

Fitness: • Health-Related Components • Warm-up
  • Cool Down

Directions: Answer the following questions in the space provided.

Question Type	Question	Answers
1. Multiple Choice	In order to gain the most benefit from flexibility exercises, what should you do first?	A. Stretch B. Drink water C. Practice hitting drills D. Warm-up
2. True or False	An appropriate warm-up in tennis should include three phases: general body warm-up, stretching, and hitting.	True or False
3. Fill in the Blank	Without a proper _____, a person could become dizzy or light-headed after exercise.	A. Cooldown B. Skilled opponent C. Diet D. Warm-up
4. Matching	Match the following activities with the associated health-related fitness component: A. One partner curls the tennis racket upwards while the other partner applies pressure downwards 10 times. B. Both partners are seated in a straddle position with feet touching. One partner pulls the other slowly and holds the position for 15 seconds. C. One player continuously alternates slide steps and jogging from sideline to sideline for 10 minutes. D. One partner uses a skinfold caliper to take measurements on a partner's triceps, abdomen, and calf.	Body composition _____ Cardio endurance _____ Flexibility _____ Muscular strength _____
5. Short Answer	Using the diagram to the left, design a cardiovascular activity that you could perform to enhance your aerobic capacity. Along with the diagram, provide a description of how you would do the activity and how it would benefit you when playing tennis. _____ _____ _____ _____	

Answer Key: (1) D   (2) True   (3) A   (4) D, C, B, A   (5) Answers will vary

(Referred to on p.15)

Figure 5. PASE Cognitive Competency Quiz – Tennis – Focus: Tennis Fitness, Quiz 2

Name: _____

PASE OUTSIDE-OF-CLASS PHYSICAL ACTIVITY PARTICIPATION LOG

Directions: Select at least four days this week in which you will participate in physical activity outside of class. Plan to do activities that will help increase your skill and fitness levels for the current sport season. Be realistic in setting your goals and planning these activities. Choose activities that you enjoy and can do with a friend or family member. Try to participate in a total of 30-60 minutes of physical activity on most, if not all, days of the week.

Scoring Criteria
❑ Planned for at least 4 days of activity by filling in the "planned columns" for each day.
❑ Performed and completed required information in the "actual column" for each day planned.
❑ Activity engaged in aided in increasing levels of fitness or skill related to the season being taught.
❑ Signed by parent or guardian and student.

In order to improve my sports skills and health, this week I plan to:

Day and Date	Physical Activity		How Long?		With Whom?		RPE	
	Planned	Actual	Planned	Actual	Planned	Actual	Planned	Actual
☑ Example 05/05/02	In-line skating	In-line skating	1/2 hour	45 min.	Alone	with brother	3	4
❑ Monday __/__/__								
❑ Tuesday __/__/__								
❑ Wednesday __/__/__								
❑ Thursday __/__/__								
❑ Friday __/__/__								
❑ Saturday __/__/__								
❑ Sunday __/__/__								

Rating of Perceived Enjoyment Scale

The activity I engage in will be/was:
4 - Extremely enjoyable
3 - Mostly enjoyable
2 - Somewhat enjoyable
1 - Not enjoyable at all

Student Signature _____

Parent/Guardian Signature _____

Teacher Signature _____

(Referred to on p.15)

Figure 6.   PASE Outside-of-Class Physical Activity Participation Log

GPAI – Ultimate

Component	Criteria
1. Decision made	Player attempts to pass to an open teammate.
2. Skill execution	Reception – Controlled pass and set-up to make a pass. Passing – disc flies level and reaches target.
3. Support	The player appeared to support the disc carrier by being in or moving to an appropriate position to receive a pass.

Team:

Name	1. Decision made		2. Skill execution		3. Support	
	A	**IA**	**E**	**IE**	**A**	**IA**
Example Student	ⅢⅢ (5)	‖ (2)	‖‖ (3)	‖‖‖ (4)	ⅢⅢ Ⅲ (8)	‖‖ (3)

Key A = Appropriate   E = Efficient
IA = Inappropriate   IE = Inefficient

Index Calculations

Game Involvement
# of appropriate decisions +
# of inappropriate decisions +
# of efficient skill executions +
# of inefficient skill executions +
# of appropriate support actions
(5 + 2 + 3 + 4 + 8 = 22)

Decision Making Index (DMI)
# of appropriate decisions /
# of inappropriate decisions
(5 ÷ 2 = 2.5)

Skill Execution Index (SEI)
# of efficient skill executions /
# of inefficient skill executions
(3 ÷ 4 = 0.75)

Support Index (SI)
# of appropriate support
actions /# of inappropriate
support actions
(8 ÷ 3 = 2.66)

Game Performance
[DMI + SEI + SI] / # of
indexes used
(2.5 + .75 + 2.66) ÷ 3 = 1.97

(Referred to on p.16)

Figure 7. GPAI – Ultimate

PASE PEER OBSERVATION SKILL CHECKLIST - THROWING

Directions: Your partner will watch you throw **5** times for each instructional cue. If the cue is performed as the picture shows, then check "**yes**"; if not then check "**no**". Add the "**yes's**" and total them at the bottom. Use the rating scale below to evaluate your throwing performance and answer the questions at the bottom of the page.

	Instructional Cue	Picture		Trial					Total "Yes"
Force Production	Side to Target		Y E S / N O	1.	2.	3.	4.	5.	**+**
	Big Step		Y E S / N O	6.	7.	8.	9.	10.	**+**
	Turn & Wrap		Y E S / N O	11.	12.	13.	14.	15.	**+**
Accuracy	Hit the Target		Y E S / N O	16.	17.	18.	19.	20.	**=**
								Total Score	

Throwing Rating Scale

❑ 0 – 8 Beginner   ❑ 9 – 15 Intermediate   ❑ 16 – 20 Advanced

What is your rating? _____

What will you do to improve your throwing force &/or accuracy?

Figure 8. PASE Peer Observation Skill Checklist – Throwing

(Referred to on p.10 & p.16)

PASE FITNESS TASK CARDS - VOLLEYBALL

Directions: With the help of the fitness trainer, select a warm-up card (A, B, or C) and complete as many of the activities (1-5) as possible during the team warm-up. Make sure to record each task on your personal recording sheet.

A		Warm-Up Card	A
HR Component		**Activity**	**Criteria**
1	CVE	Run/jog continuously from the baseline to the net and back again.	3 minutes
2	MSE	Holding a volleyball between your hands, perform partner-resisted arm curls.	2 x 15 reps
3	FLX	Reach one arm across your chest and use the other arm to pull on the elbow until you feel a stretch in the back of the shoulder. Repeat the stretch for the opposite arm.	Hold 30 sec.
4	MSE	With a partner, one on each side of the net, mirror one another as you perform the skill of blocking up and down the length of the net.	2x up and back
5	FLX	Sitting on the floor, spread your legs in a straddle position. Lean to one side and reach for your ankle. Repeat to the opposite side.	Hold 30 sec.

B		Warm-Up Card	B
HR Component		**Activity**	**Criteria**
1	CVE	Run/jog continuously around the outside of the volleyball court.	3 minutes
2	MSE	While holding a volleyball, perform abdominal curl-ups on a floor mat. Raise the ball to touch your partner's hands.	1 set of as many reps as possible
3	FLX	Complete a hurdler's stretch for your right and left legs.	Hold 30 sec.
4	MSE	Perform walking lunges from the baseline to the net and back again.	2x up and back
5	FLX	While sitting, have your legs flexed and spread with your heels touching. Pull your feet toward you while pushing knees to floor.	Hold 30 sec.

C		Warm-Up Card	C
HR Component		**Activity**	**Criteria**
1	CVE	Jump rope continuously.	3 min.
2	MSE	Perform push-ups by placing a volleyball underneath your chest and lowering your body each time to touch the ball before rising.	2 x 15 reps
3	FLX	Reach your spiking arm over your shoulder on the same side, trying to grab the opposite hand behind your back. Repeat w/ both arms.	Hold 15 sec.
4	MSE	Perform squats with a volleyball. Hold the ball, squat, place the ball on the ground, stand up, squat, pick up ball, and repeat.	2 x 15 reps
5	FLX	Sitting on the floor, spread your legs in a straddle position. Lean to one side and reach for your ankle. Repeat to the opposite side.	Hold 30 sec.

(Referred to on p.8 & p.17)

Figure 9. PASE Fitness Task Cards – Volleyball

Name: _____

PASE FITNESS RECORDING SHEET - DAILY, PRE, & POST – VOLLEYBALL

Directions: To begin each lesson, select a warm-up: A, B, or C. Circle your choice and check off each activity as you complete it. After the warm-up, note your effort level by checking the indicators that apply to you.

Lessons

Warm-Up Activities	3	4	5	6	7	8	9	10	11
	A B C	A B C	A B C	A B C	A B C	A B C	A B C	A B C	A B C
1	☐	☐	☐	☐	☐	☐	☐	☐	☐
2	☐	☐	☐	☐	☐	☐	☐	☐	☐
3	☐	☐	☐	☐	☐	☐	☐	☐	☐
4	☐	☐	☐	☐	☐	☐	☐	☐	☐
5	☐	☐	☐	☐	☐	☐	☐	☐	☐

Effort Level

	3	4	5	6	7	8	9	10	11
Flush Face?	☐	☐	☐	☐	☐	☐	☐	☐	☐
Sweating?	☐	☐	☐	☐	☐	☐	☐	☐	☐
Breathing Hard?	☐	☐	☐	☐	☐	☐	☐	☐	☐

Lessons

Warm-Up Activities	12	13	14	15	16	17	18	19	20
	A B C	A B C	A B C	A B C	A B C	A B C	A B C	A B C	A B C
1	☐	☐	☐	☐	☐	☐	☐	☐	☐
2	☐	☐	☐	☐	☐	☐	☐	☐	☐
3	☐	☐	☐	☐	☐	☐	☐	☐	☐
4	☐	☐	☐	☐	☐	☐	☐	☐	☐
5	☐	☐	☐	☐	☐	☐	☐	☐	☐

Effort Level

	12	13	14	15	16	17	18	19	20
Flush Face?	☐	☐	☐	☐	☐	☐	☐	☐	☐
Sweating?	☐	☐	☐	☐	☐	☐	☐	☐	☐
Breathing Hard?	☐	☐	☐	☐	☐	☐	☐	☐	☐

Directions: **For Lesson 2:** Note your pre-test scores for the pre-season fitness test in the column marked "Pre-Test Scores." Set personal goals immediately after completing each test.

For Lesson 21: Note your post-test scores for the post-season fitness test in the column marked "Post-Test Scores."

Health-Related Fitness Components and Tests	Pre-Test Scores (Lesson 2)	Goals	Post-Test Scores (Lesson 21)
Cardiovascular Endurance • _____			
Muscular Strength & Endurance • _____ • _____			
Flexibility • _____ • _____			
Body Composition • _____			

Figure 10. PASE Fitness Recording Sheet – Daily, Pre & Post – Volleyball

(Referred to on p.8 & p.17)

Name: _____

PASE ROLE AND RESPONSIBILITIES CHECKLIST – DANCE

Directions:	Use the shading to determine your role and corresponding responsibilities for the day's lesson. At the end of the lesson you will be asked to determine the responsibilities that you successfully completed. For each responsibility successfully completed, place a check [✔] in the box. For each responsibility that you did not successfully complete, place a zero [0] in the box. If you are the choreographer, then your role will not rotate and you will perform the choreographer role for the entire season. All other roles will rotate on a regular basis as denoted by the shaded areas.

Roles and Responsibilities

Roles and Responsibilities	Lesson 1	2	3	4	5	6	7	8	9	10	11	12
Choreographer												
• Leads dance troupe practice	✔											
• Assists teacher when needed	0											
• Assists teammates in learning dance moves	✔											
Fitness Trainer												
• Selects appropriate warm-up activities		▨						▨				
• Leads troupe warm-up		▨						▨				
• Reports injuries to teacher		▨						▨				
• Aids teacher in administering first-aid		▨						▨				
Dance Season Committee Member												
• Assists in selecting dance troupes			▨						▨			
• Summarizes the application dance scores			▨						▨			
• Monitors allotted dance times during contests			▨						▨			
• Judges Dance Fever application tasks			▨						▨			
Disc Jockey (DJ)												
• Maintains and monitors audio equipment				▨						▨		
• Chooses appropriate music for troupe routines				▨						▨		
• Records team strategy practice				▨						▨		
Master of Ceremonies												
• Introduces troupe members, dance themes, and musical selections					▨						▨	
• Attends to management of practice and application tasks					▨						▨	
Reviewer/Critic												
• Publicizes records via newsletters, etc.						▨						▨
• Reports progress daily to troupe members						▨						▨
• Assumes role responsibilities for absent troupe members						▨						▨

(Referred to on p.17)

Figure 11. PASE Role and Reponsibilities Checklist – Dance

PASE ETIQUETTE CHECKLIST - GOLF

Directions: Determine if you successfully completed the etiquette indicators while on the tee box, the fairway, and the green. After completing the checklist for holes 1-9, you and your partner should sign at the bottom of the page to indicate that the checklist is accurate. Next, determine your overall etiquette rating for 9 holes played and answer the two questions at the bottom of the page.

Etiquette Indicators	Ex	1	2	3	4	5	6	7	8	9
On the Tee Box the Golfer…										
• Waited until the group ahead was clearly out of range before teeing off.	✔									
• With lowest score on previous hole teed off first (honors).	✔									
• Not teeing off stood well behind and to the side of golfer who was teeing off.	✔									
• Not teeing off refrained from talking or swinging while others were teeing off.	✔									
• Repaired divot after teeing off.	✖									
On the Fairway the Golfer…										
• Kept pace with group ahead.	✔									
• Looked for lost ball(s) for no more than 5 min.	✔									
• Warned other golfers of an errant shot by yelling "fore."	✔									
• Repaired all divots after hitting.	✖									
• Farthest away from the green played his/her shot first.	✔									
• Raked sand traps of divot and feet marks.	✔									
On the Green the Golfer…										
• Placed bag just off of the green.	✔									
• Avoided walking in other golfer's putting line.	✔									
• Did not drag feet when walking on green, especially if wearing spiked shoes.	✔									
• Repaired all ball marks on green immediately.	✔									
• Closest to hole attended to the flagstick.	✔									
• Replaced flagstick and proceeded to next tee box before marking scores.	✔									

Golf Holes

Scoring Key: ✔ Golfer performed this action successfully. ✖ Golfer did not perform this action successfully.

Your Signature_____ Partner's Signature_____

Golf Etiquette Rating Scale for 9 Holes

❑ Birdie 0 – 2 X's ❑ Par 3 – 5 X's ❑ Bogey 6 – 8 X's ❑ Double Bogey 9+ X's

What is your golf etiquette rating for all 9 holes? _____

What will you do to improve your golfing etiquette in the future? _____

Figure 12. PASE Etiquette Checklist – Golf

(Referred to on p.17)

PASE RESPONSIBLE SPORTSPERSON PLEDGE

We, _____ (Team Name)

agree to:

- Always follow the rules
- Respect the officials' decisions
- Be gracious in victory and defeat
- Show self-control at all times

- Work to achieve our personal and team goals
- Encourage all of our classmates
- Assist our teammates at any time
- Play hard and fair

Each team member should write the following phrase in one of the boxes below and sign and date. Please write as legibly as possible.

Pledge Phrase: *As part of this team, I promise to always follow the criteria outlined in the Responsible Sportsperson Pledge. Should I choose not to follow the pledge, I understand that there are consequences that my team and I must deal with in a responsible fashion.*

Copy Pledge Phrase Below	Sign & Date
	_____ / __ / __ Sportsperson _____ / __ / __ Teacher
	_____ / __ / __ Sportsperson _____ / __ / __ Teacher
	_____ / __ / __ Sportsperson _____ / __ / __ Teacher

(Referred to on p.18)

Figure 13. PASE Responsible Sportsperson Pledge

Name: _____

PASE COGNITIVE LITERACY QUIZ – FLAG FOOTBALL		

- **Rules, Roles, and Rituals**

Directions: Answer the following questions in the space provided.

Question Type	Question	Answers
1. Multiple Choice	The following explanation illustrates which violation? After the quarterback has thrown the ball, a player impedes the progress of an opponent who has a chance to catch the pass.	A. Encroachment B. Pass interference C. Illegal motion D. Holding
2. True or False	It is legal for a running back who has crossed the line of scrimmage to throw a forward pass to a receiver downfield.	True or False
3. Fill in the Blank	_____ is typically used to start a regulation game of flag football. This tradition helps to determine which team will kickoff and which team will receive the ball to begin the game.	A. Handshake B. Jump ball C. Coin toss D. Face off
4. Matching	Match the following responsibilities with their corresponding role: A. Manages and interprets the rules of the contest while mediating any conflicts that may arise. B. Leads skill and strategy practice for the players who are involved in advancing the ball to score. C. Reports injuries to the teacher and aids teacher in administering first-aid and safety. D. Leads skill and strategy practice for the players who are involved in stopping the advancement of the ball into their area of the field.	Offensive coach_____ Defensive coach _____ Fitness trainer_____ Official _____
5. Short Answer	In the space provided below, list three rituals that your team has developed for the following segments of a flag football game: • Pre Game: _____ _____ • Halftime: _____ _____ • Post Game: _____ _____	

Answer Key: **(1)** B **(2)** False **(3)** C **(4)** B, D, C, A **(5)** Answers will vary

(Referred to on p.18)

Figure 14. PASE Cognitive Literacy Quiz – Flag Football

PASE REFLECTIVE JOURNAL

Directions: Answer the questions below completely. Your responses should be related specifically to the lessons that have passed since your last journal entry. To receive full credit for your journal entry, be sure to address each area of the scoring criteria. Journal writings will be assigned during weeks 1, 3, and 5 and are due at the end of the week assigned.

Scoring Criteria
❑ Answered each question completely and honestly. ❑ Provided specific, personal examples from physical education class to support answers. ❑ Used proper grammar and punctuation.

Questions

1 During the past week(s) you have participated in a variety of different roles. You were required to plan for and organize certain aspects of the sport education season.
- Describe the parts of the season you planned for and organized. In what ways did your plans work or not work?
- With what level of responsibility do you feel you completed your planning and organizational duties? Why?
- How would you plan differently in the future?
- What role did you enjoy most? Why?

2 In the various roles that you have engaged in as part of the sport season, you have provided leadership.
- Describe one way in which you have displayed leadership to your team, to another team, or to the whole class.
- How did this experience make you feel?
- What can you do to become a better leader?

3 Throughout the season your team has developed many goals.
- List one goal that your team has set and achieved.
- Provide an explanation as to how you and your teammates accomplished this goal.
- Describe how meeting this goal made you feel.
- List a goal that your team has set and has not yet achieved.
- Provide an explanation of what is preventing your team from meeting that goal.
- Describe how not yet meeting this goal has made you feel.

4 Your team has developed many rituals during this sport season.
- Describe a unique ritual that you and your teammates have created during this sport season.
- Why is this an appropriate ritual for this particular sport season?
- Compare and contrast the ritual your team created with those of other teams.

5 Think back to a situation during the season when you feel you may have been treated unfairly.
- List who was involved in the situation and describe why you believe the incident occurred.
- How did you handle this incident?
- How did this incident make you feel?
- How could this issue have been handled to create a more positive outcome?

(Referred to on p.9 & p.19)

Figure 15. PASE Reflective Journal

PASE INDIVIDUAL RESPONSIBILITY LEVEL (IRL) RUBRIC

Directions: Use the rubric below to determine your individual level of responsibility for each lesson. Record your individual responsibility level on the Individual Responsibility Level Recording Sheet.

Exemplary

4

Preparedness	You were on time for class and prepared with appropriate clothes, shoes, and materials.
Transition	You always stopped, cleaned up, and moved to the next lesson segment as efficiently as possible.
On-Task	You were always engaged at a high level during practice and game times, and you tried your best.
Sportsmanship	You maintained a positive attitude throughout all daily activities and displayed good sportsmanship.
Assessments	You completed all of the team and individual assessments during the lesson completely and honestly.

Acceptable

3

Preparedness	You were late for class but came prepared with appropriate clothes, shoes, and materials.
Transition	You stopped, cleaned up, and moved to the next lesson segment as efficiently as possible for most of the lesson.
On-Task	You engaged at a high level during practice and game times for most of the lesson, but there were times you did not try your best.
Sportsmanship	You maintained a positive attitude throughout most daily activities and displayed good sportsmanship.
Assessments	You completed most of the team and individual assessments during the lesson completely and honestly.

Needs Improvement

2

Preparedness	You were on time for class but did not come prepared with appropriate clothes, shoes, and materials.
Transition	You rarely stopped, cleaned up, and moved to the next lesson segment as efficiently as possible.
On-Task	You rarely engaged at a high level during practice and game times, and there were times you did not try your best.
Sportsmanship	You maintained a negative attitude throughout most daily activities or displayed poor sportsmanship.
Assessments	You completed most of the team and individual assessments during the lesson, but the information was not complete or honest.

Unacceptable

1

Preparedness	You were late for class and did not come prepared with appropriate clothes, shoes, and materials.
Transition	You never stopped, cleaned up, and moved to the next lesson segment as efficiently as possible.
On-Task	You were never engaged at a high level during practice and game times, and you did not try your best.
Sportsmanship	You maintained a negative attitude throughout all daily activities and displayed poor sportsmanship.
Assessments	You did not complete any of the team and individual assessments during the lesson.

(Referred to on p.19)

Figure 16. PASE Individual Responsibility Level (IRL) Rubric

Name: _____

PASE INDIVIDUAL RESPONSIBILITY LEVEL (IRL) RECORDING SHEET

Directions: Determine your individual responsibility level (IRL) for each lesson using the individual responsibility rubric. Record your score in the "IRL" column and provide a rationale for why you were at that level. Set an IRL goal for the next lesson and develop a strategy for meeting that goal. Complete a written reflection after lessons 7, 14, and 20 by responding to questions A, B, and C.

A. Calculate and list the number of times you were at each level during the lessons since your last written reflection.

B. For each level you demonstrated, summarize the decisions you made to place yourself at that level of responsibility.

C. What strategies can you use to maintain or improve your level of responsibility both in and outside of PE in the future?

Lesson	IRL	Reason Why?	IRL Goal	Strategy for Improvement
Ex.	1	I forgot my shoes. I got mad and yelled at Sue because she wouldn't pass me the ball.	2	I will leave a pair of shoes in my locker and I'll ask Sue to pass to me.
1				
2				
3				
4				
5				
6				
7				
8				
9				
10				
11				
12				
13				
14				
15				
16				
17				
18				
19				
20				
21				

(Referred to on p.19)

Figure 17. PASE Individual Responsibility Level (IRL) Recording Sheet

PASE EVENT TASKS

Directions: Your team must complete the event task as described. Use the scoring rubric at the bottom of the page to help your team plan for and monitor your progress while completing the event task. Although there are a variety of ways to plan for and perform the event tasks, each team will be evaluated using the same scoring rubric.

Event Task 1 – Grade 12

Your team has been asked to organize a station as part of a sports clinic for upper elementary and middle school students in your district. The clinic will require you to teach one skill or strategy that you are learning during the current sport education season. Identify the skill or strategy that you will teach and develop a plan for teaching this information to the elementary and middle school children. Develop and assign individual roles to each member of your team for the clinic. Make sure the responsibilities for each role are clearly defined so that each team member understands his/her specific job for the clinic. The clinic will last 40 minutes.

Event Task 2 – Grade 10

Your team's assignment is to create a script for a play about social acceptance within a sporting context. Create a play that demonstrates your team's understanding of and respect for others during game play. Identify each of the roles that will be included in your play. Within your play develop an example of appropriate and inappropriate interactions that might possibly take place during game play. Possible sporting issues that your play can include, but are not limited to are: (a) acceptance of others from different cultures, (b) the inclusion of students with special needs, or (c) playing with students who have differing levels of skill. Each team member should have some part in the planning and acting out of your play. The play will last 7-10 minutes.

Event Task 3 – Grade 8

Your team has been chosen to develop an awards banquet to bring the end of the sport season to a festive close. In planning for the banquet your team must determine the awards to be given and the criteria for each award. As you plan for the awards banquet, remember that each person from every team should receive an award of some kind. Your team must also create an itinerary for the banquet, plan for and invite a quest speaker, and develop a healthy-refreshment menu. The awards banquet will last 30 minutes.

Scoring Rubric for Event Tasks

4 = Exemplary
- Provided complete and comprehensive rationale for decisions the team made when planning.
- All team members were included, and each had a defined role.
- All social interactions were positive; no conflicts when planning.
- All ideas from team members were accepted or given equal consideration.

3 = Acceptable
- Provided complete and comprehensive rationale for most decisions the team made when planning.
- Most team members were included, and most had a defined role.
- Most social interactions were positive; any minor conflicts were resolved when planning.
- Most ideas from team members were accepted or given equal consideration.

2 = Needs Improvement
- Provided incomplete rationales for decisions the team made when planning.
- Several people on the team were not included, and several roles were not clearly defined.
- Most social interactions were negative; some conflicts remained unresolved.
- Most ideas from team members were not accepted or given equal consideration.

1 = Unacceptable
- Provided no rationales for the decisions the team made when planning.
- Most team members were not included, and no roles were clearly defined.
- All social interactions were negative; most conflicts remained unresolved.
- All ideas from team members were not accepted or given equal consideration.

Figure 18. PASE Event Tasks

(Referred to on p.19)

PASE INDEPENDENT LEARNING ACTIVITY

Directions: Select one of the following roles that you would like to perform within the local community (i.e., the recreation center, the YMCA, etc.), for an afternoon. As you determine your choice, note that the criteria for each role are similar to responsibilities that you performed for these roles in PE. As you complete the optional role, check off each criterion. Once you have completed the optional role, summarize your experiences.

Optional Role Choices and Criteria

Manager
- ❏ Inspected and cared for equipment
- ❏ Distributed and collected equipment
- ❏ Monitored participants' performance
- ❏ Assumed administrative duties assigned
- ❏ Monitored time of activities
- ❏ Organized practice/game space

Trainer
- ❏ Selected appropriate warm-up activities
- ❏ Led/monitored warm-up activities
- ❏ Reported injuries to appropriate personnel
- ❏ Aided in administering first-aid if needed

Reporter
- ❏ Selected one player from each team to interview following the sporting event
- ❏ Acquired statistics
- ❏ Selected one coach to interview following the sporting event
- ❏ Write a 1/2-page sports column

Summary of Experience

Directions: Write a summary of your optional role experience. Use the scoring rubric at the bottom of the page to help you write the summary. Provide an explanation of how you chose your role, explain how you prepared to complete your role to criteria, and describe how you met each criterion associated with your role.

Scoring Rubric

4 = Exemplary
- Fully explained role choice and plan for completing role.
- Completed all responsibilities associated with the selected role.
- Explained each role responsibility, provided specific examples.

3 = Acceptable
- Mostly explained role choice and plan for completing role.
- Completed most of the responsibilities associated with the selected role.
- Explained most of the responsibilities, provided examples.

2 = Needs Improvement
- Vaguely explained role choice and plan for completing role.
- Completed few of the responsibilities associated with the selected role.
- Explained a few of the responsibilities, used few examples.

1 = Unacceptable
- Did not explain role choice or plan for completing role.
- Did not complete any of the responsibilities associated with the selected role.
- Did not explain any of the responsibilities or provide any examples.

(Referred to on p.20)

Figure 19. PASE Independent Learning Activity

PART 6

Grading in Sport Education

Assessment is used for many specific purposes in physical education including the determination of student grades. Most teachers are charged with the responsibility of grading. Grades are intended to quantify student progress and should be derived from sound assessment practices. Unfortunately, many physical education teachers determine student grades from nonperformance-related variables such as attire, attendance, and attitude. These grading practices represent an area of significant concern for the physical education profession, especially during a time of heightened emphasis on student outcomes and accountability in education. Sound grading practices for physical education should be based primarily on student performance related to predetermined educational goals.

If used appropriately, grades represent the ultimate student accountability system. Siedentop (1994) indicates, "most sport education programs have worked well because teachers have developed clear accountability systems for student performance" (p. 33). If grading systems are to be meaningful for students they must be clear, aligned with program goals, and shared with learners prior to instruction (Siedentop & Tannehill, 2000). Physical education teachers can design meaningful grading systems for a sport education seasons by (a) determining appropriate student learning outcomes, (b) establishing criteria for sufficient performance for each outcome, and (c) developing strategies for assessing each outcome.

Because the grading system should be shared with students at the beginning of a season, we suggest using a "student syllabus" like the sample represented in Figure 20 on pages 41 and 42. A student syllabus clearly communicates the teacher's expectations and provides an overview of the entire season. The following items are commonly included in a PASE season syllabus: (a) general description

of the season, (b) learning goals, (c) content, (d) requirements, (e) grading scheme, and (f) daily calendar.

A well-designed student syllabus provides students with a brief summary of the planned learning activities within a season. This description provides an advance organizer for the season and heightens student awareness and expectation for what lies ahead. Next, the syllabus describes the seasonal goals. By clearly communicating goals at the start of the season, students are more likely to understand, work towards, and achieve the season goals. The season content section of the syllabus specifically identifies the skills and tactics that students can expect to learn as a result of participating in the season. This content outline serves to heighten student motivation in anticipation of learning the skills and tactics for a specific sport or activity.

A syllabus also includes the requirements for the season, the point value for each requirement, and the overall grading scale. By providing this information, students are better able to meet the prescribed season requirements, as well as understand the value of each requirement in relation to the overall grading scale. A season calendar outlines the type and timing of assessment to be used on a day-to-day basis throughout the season. This component of the syllabus supplies students with the information necessary for adequately preparing for each class in advance. In addition, the calendar provides students with a means for monitoring their personal progress throughout the season. Finally, the season requirements are briefly described. This section provides an overview of each requirement and also enables students to prepare for class on a daily basis. As the season progresses, however, additional handouts and/or instructions would be necessary for students to successfully complete many of the season requirements.

Name: _____

PASE SOCCER SEASON SYLLABUS

Instructor(s): Mr. Robert & Mrs. Waronsky
Class: PE 101 – Freshman PE
Time: Monday – Friday 12:30 – 2:00

Soccer Season Description	This soccer season consists of 25 lessons and is divided into 3 segments: a pre season, an in-season round robin tournament, and a post-season championship tournament. Throughout the season, each student will be responsible for performing various tasks related to playing and managing a soccer season. Good luck!

Season Goals

To become...

- A **competent** soccer player.   One who is a knowledgeable player and can successfully perform skills and strategies during a soccer game.
- A **literate** soccer player.   One who knows the rules and traditions of the sport and can identify appropriate and inappropriate soccer behaviors.
- An **enthusiastic** soccer player.   One who is involved and behaves in ways that protect, preserve, and enhance the culture of soccer.

Season Content

Skills (What to do)		Tactics (How to use skills)	
❖ Dribbling	❖ Trapping	❖ Preventing the turn	❖ Overlap
❖ Passing	❖ Goal Keeping	❖ Delay	❖ Crossover
❖ Shooting	❖ Marking & Covering	❖ Clearing	❖ Distribution

Season Requirements, Points, & Grading Scale

Requirement		Point Value			
✎	Activity Tasks Cards	10	@	1	=	10
⚊	Personal Fitness Assessment	18	@	1	=	18
▦	Pre & Post Fitness & Skills Combine	2	@	3	=	6
♥♥♥	Outside-of-PE Participation Log	5	@	1	=	5
🎭	Role Performance	21	@	1	=	21
☖	Individual Responsibility	24	@	1	=	24
📄	Written Quizzes	3	@	2	=	6
🏆	End-of-Season Awards Voting	1	@	2	=	2
☺	Reflective Journal	5	@	1	=	5
ⓘ	Independent Learning Activity	1	@	3	=	3
				Total	=	100

Grading Scale		
A	95 – 100	Excellent
A-	93 – 94	
B+	91 – 92	Above Average
B	87 – 90	
B-	85 – 86	
C+	83 – 84	Average
C	79 – 82	
C-	77 – 78	
D+	75 – 76	Below Average
D	72 – 74	
D-	70 – 71	
F	Below 70	Failing

📖 **Team Portfolio**   **Must be turned in before final grade can be calculated.**

✚ **Season Bonus Points**				
Added to final point total	1st place = 3 points	4th place = 1.5 points
	2nd place = 2.5 points	5th place = 1 point
	3rd place = 2 points	6th place = 0.5 point

(Referred to on p.40)

Figure 20. PASE Soccer Season Syllabus (page 1)

Name: _____

PASE SOCCER SEASON SYLLABUS

Directions: Record your personal progress each day. As you complete a requirement, check it off like this: "☑"

Season Calendar & Daily Assessments		Pre Season															In-Season Round Robin						Post Season			
	Lesson	1	2	3	4	5	6	7	8	9	10	11	12	13	14	15	16	17	18	19	20	21	22	23	24	25
	Date																									
✍				❑	❑	❑		❑	❑	❑		❑	❑	❑		❑										
♟				❑	❑	❑	❑	❑	❑	❑	❑	❑	❑	❑	❑	❑	❑	❑	❑	❑	❑					
▦		❑																				❑				
♟♟♟							❑					❑					❑					❑				❑
🎴				❑	❑	❑	❑	❑	❑	❑	❑	❑	❑	❑	❑	❑	❑	❑	❑	❑	❑		❑	❑	❑	
✋			❑	❑	❑	❑	❑	❑	❑	❑	❑	❑	❑	❑	❑	❑	❑	❑	❑	❑	❑	❑	❑	❑	❑	
📄		❑											❑									❑				
🏆																									❑	
☺							❑					❑					❑					❑				❑
ⓘ																										❑
📖																										❑
✛																										pts

Requirement Descriptions			
✍	Activity Tasks Cards	A series of skill and strategy development activities that must be completed by individual team members during team practice in lessons 3-5, 7-9, 11-13, and 15.
♟	Personal Fitness Assessment	A set of fitness development activities that are completed and results recorded during the team warm-up portion of lessons 3-20.
▦	Pre & Post Fitness & Skills Combine	A variety of stations designed to provide pre- and post-season information for goal setting and monitoring of personal progress between lessons 1 and 21.
♟♟♟	Outside-of-PE Participation Log	An activity designed to provide additional opportunities for students to engage in meaningful physical activity outside of the PE class throughout the soccer season.
🎴	Role Performance	A performance of roles designed to help manage the soccer season. Daily roles and responsibilities are carried out in lessons 3-20 and 22-24.
✋	Individual Responsibility	A reflective activity used for identifying and monitoring one's personal behaviors throughout the soccer season. To be completed at the end of lessons 2-24.
📄	Written Quizzes	A series of written activities used to determine one's knowledge of soccer. In-class and/or take-home quizzes will be given on lessons 1, 12, and 21.
🏆	End-of-Season Awards Voting	A voting activity used to identify individual accomplishments on and off of the soccer field throughout the season. Voting to be completed in lesson 24.
☺	Reflective Journal	An activity used to promote critical thinking by exploring issues related to participation in the soccer season. Completed on lessons 6, 11, 16, 21, and 25.
ⓘ	Independent Learning Activity	An activity used to give students the opportunity to transfer what is being learned in PE to other physical activity situations. To be completed by lesson 25.
📖	Team Portfolio	Teams will compile and organize all individual and team documents in a binder. The portfolio must be turned in on lesson 25 before final grades can be calculated.
✛	Season Bonus Points	Throughout the season individuals will earn points for their team. Points will be acquired from application contest scores, superior role performances, and demonstration of exemplary sport behaviors. Points are accumulated on a daily basis and will be used to determine the overall season champions. Individuals will receive bonus points added to his/her grade according to final team standings.

(Referred to on p.40)

Figure 20. PASE Soccer Season Syllabus (page 2)

## PART 7

Assessment of the Teaching-Learning Environment in Sport Education

Assessment in sport education fulfills many important purposes or needs (see Table 2, page 11). Each of the previously described assessment practices can be used to address a variety of these specific educational purposes. In addition to providing valuable information regarding student progress, a number of these assessment strategies indirectly monitor the quality of the actual teaching-learning environment. A well-crafted set of reflective journal questions, for example, directly informs the teacher about student perceptions and indirectly provides the teacher with comments about the effectiveness of certain process-related aspects of a lesson or season.

It is important to understand and appreciate the direct and indirect purposes of these assessment strategies in relation to the establishment of an effective teaching-learning environment. Due to the relative complexity of a sport education season, more focused methods of assessment may be needed to directly measure the effectiveness of the educational process at several points across a season.

Within a typical PASE lesson, both the teacher and the student regularly carry out important instructional and managerial functions. The quality with which these basic functions are performed ultimately determines the effectiveness of the teaching-learning environment. To ensure efficient and effective implementation of the sport education model, a teacher can use the PASE Teacher Observation Instrument and the PASE Student Observation Instrument to directly monitor the quality of the employed instructional process.

Instrument: PASE Teacher & Student Observation Instruments (Figures 21 and 22, pages 45 and 46)

Purpose: Both observation instruments provide the teacher with a method for directly monitoring the quality of the teaching-learning environment during a lesson. In order to ensure that the sport education model is being properly implemented, it is important for the teacher to evaluate his/her instructional behaviors in combination with the associated student behaviors during each component of the lesson. The process-related data collected through this type of structured observation can then be used to improve the effectiveness of the teaching-learning environment.

When to Implement: Both observation instruments should be used on a regular basis in order to obtain a clear representation of the overall effectiveness of the teaching-learning environment. Although there is not an established standard, we suggest using each observation instrument at least five times during the season. The more frequently the observation instruments are used to monitor student and teacher behavior the better.

How to Implement: The observation instruments can be used in a variety of ways including direct observation and/or by videotaped observation of the teaching-learning environment. Irrespective of the way in which they are implemented, observers should be trained to use the instruments in order to ensure consistent and accurate results. Both the teacher and student observation instruments require the observer to rate the behaviors of the teacher or student depending on which instrument is being used.

During each lesson component, the observer determines the quality of the action observed on a scale from four to one, with four being exemplary and one being unacceptable. Next the observer records the rating and notes strategies for maintaining or improving the ratings associated with each lesson component. As the lesson progresses, the observer continues to watch for, rate, and record the quality of each action.

During a direct observation, a fellow physical education teacher or school administrator, can observe the lesson and code the teacher or student actions accordingly. A teacher can also conduct a self-assessment by viewing a videotaped lesson. If a teacher chooses this method for collecting data, he/she needs to take appropriate measures to ensure the quality of the videotaping process. These quality assurance measures include: (a) inspecting the video equipment prior to taping the lesson; (b) using the widest camera angle to capture as much of the teaching-learning environment as possible; and (c) placing the video recorder in a secure position so that the safety of the students is not jeopardized. Both methods of observation have proven to be equally effective for providing teachers with important feedback related to maintaining and improving the effectiveness of their teaching-learning environment during a sport education season.

PASE TEACHER OBSERVATION INSTRUMENT

Teacher_____   Observer_____   Date_____

Lesson Focus_____   Class_____

Directions: Rate each teacher action according to the scale at the bottom of the page and note comments.

Lesson Component	Rating	Teacher Actions	Comments
Daily Role & Responsibility Check	_____ _____	Provided list of role responsibilities Monitored environment	
Team Warm-Up & Student-Coach's Meeting	_____ _____ _____	Provided warm-up activities Provided student-coaching plan Conducted student-coach's meeting	
Skill/Tactics Review	_____ _____ _____	Indirectly facilitated review Monitored environment Focused teams when necessary	
Skill/Tactics Instruction	_____ _____ _____	Oriented learners to new skills & tactics Reviewed previous skills & tactics Conducted whole-class guided drills	
Team Practice	_____ _____ _____ _____	Provided learning activities Indirectly facilitated practice Monitored environment Focused teams when necessary	
Application Contest	_____ _____ _____ _____	Designed contest to apply daily skills/tactics Provided statistics recording sheet Advised referees Managed contest	
Lesson Closure	_____ _____ _____ _____ _____ _____	Refocused on & reviewed skills/tactics Questioned students Allowed for demonstrations Provided feedback on students' progress Previewed upcoming lesson Supplied out-of-class assignments	
Individual & Team Progress Report	_____ _____	Provided assessment documents Monitored record-keeping procedures	

Rating Scale		
4 = Exemplary	Action occurred with exceptional quality	
3 = Acceptable	Action occurred with adequate quality	
2 = Needs Improvement	Action occurred, but with marginal quality	
1 = Unacceptable	Action did not occur	

(Referred to on p.43)

Figure 21. PASE Teacher Observation Instrument

PASE STUDENT OBSERVATION INSTRUMENT

Student/Team_____   Observer_____   Date_____

Lesson Focus_____   Class_____

Directions:	Rate each student action according to the scale at the bottom of the page and note comments.		

Lesson Component	Rating	Student/Team Actions	Comments
Daily Role & Responsibility Check	_____ _____	Identified daily roles Prepared for warm-up or student-coach's meeting	
Team Warm-Up & Student-Coach's Meeting	_____ _____ _____	Fitness trainer led team warm-up Teammates engaged in warm-up Student-coaches met with teacher	
Skill/Tactics Review	Student-coach... _____ _____ _____ Teammates... _____	Directed team review Monitored individual's progress on goals Monitored team's progress on goals Engaged in review drills	
Skill/Tactics Instruction	_____ _____ _____ _____	Observed teacher Asked/answered questions Engaged in demonstrations Participated in intro/review drills	
Team Practice	Student-coach... _____ _____ Teammates... _____	Directed team practice Monitored team's progress on activities Engaged in practice drills	
Application Contest	_____ _____ _____ _____	Student-coach prepped team for contest Statisticians recorded contest statistics Officials refereed contest Players participated in contest	
Lesson Closure	_____ _____ _____	Observed teacher Asked/answered questions Engaged in demonstrations	
Individual & Team Progress Report	_____ _____	Collected, organized, summarized, & recorded team progress on goals Collected, organized, summarized, & individual progress on goals	
Rating Scale	4 = Exemplary 3 = Acceptable 2 = Needs Improvement 1 = Unacceptable	Action occurred with exceptional quality Action occurred with adequate quality Action occurred, but with marginal quality Action did not occur	

(Referred to on p.43)

Figure 22. PASE Student Observation Instrument

CONCLUSION

The purpose of this document was to describe the important role that assessment plays in sport education. Ultimately, assessment in sport education is used to inform students, teachers, parents, administrators, and the like about learners' progress towards becoming competent, literate, and enthusiastic sportspersons. Since the sport education model is gaining considerable support as an effective approach for teaching sport in school-based physical education programs, it is critical that appropriate strategies for assessing students be established.

As previously discussed, the use of frequent and authentic forms of assessment remains a defining characteristic of the sport education model. The conceptual framework for assessing student outcomes in sport education provided in this document is intended to serve as a guide for physical educators who are beginning the exciting and rewarding process of implementing sport education in the classes they teach. The sample assessment instruments and associated learning activities described herein represent just a few of the possibilities available for documenting, monitoring, and enhancing student learning during a sport education season. As familiarity with sport education increases, physical educators will only be limited by their creativity in exploring unique and highly individualized methods for assessing the progress of their students and their own instructional effectiveness.

REFERENCES

Alexander, K., Taggart, A., & Luckman, J. (1998). Pilgrims progress: The sport education crusade down under. *Journal of Physical Education, Recreation, & Dance, 69*(4), 21-23.

Carlson, T., & Hastie, P. (1997). The student social system within sport education. *Journal of Teaching in Physical Education, 16*(2), 176-183.

Collier, C. (1998). Sport education and preservice education. *Journal of Physical Education, Recreation, & Dance, 69*(5), 44-45.

Graves, M.A., Mohr, D.J., Wiegand, R.L., & Nolan, C. (2000). The effect of sport education curricular preparation on the curricular behavior of PETE students. *Research Quarterly for Exercise and Sport, 71* (Suppl. 1), A-70.

Graves, M.A., & Townsend, J.S. (2000). Applying the sport education curriculum model to dance. *Journal of Physical Education, Recreation, & Dance, 71*(8), 50-54.

Griffin, L., Mitchell, S., & Oslin, J. (1997). *Teaching sport concepts and skills: A tactical games approach.* Champaign, IL: Human Kinetics.

Hastad, D., & Lacy, A. (1998). *Measurement and evaluation in physical education and exercise science* (3rd ed.). Boston, MA: Allyn & Bacon.

Hastie, P. (1998) Applied benefits of the sport education model. *Journal of Physical Education, Recreation, & Dance, 69*(4), 24-26.

Mohr, D. J., Townsend, J. S., & Bulger, S. M. (2001). A pedagogical approach to sport education season planning. *Journal of Physical Education, Recreation, & Dance, 72*(9), 37-46.

Mohr, D. J., Townsend, J. S., & Bulger, S. M. (2002). Maintaining the PASE: A day in the life of sport education. *Journal of Physical Education, Recreation, & Dance, 73*(1), 36-44.

National Association for Sport and Physical Education. (1995). *Moving into the future: National standards for physical education.* Reston, VA: WCB McGraw-Hill.

Siedentop, D. (1994). *Quality PE through positive sport experiences: Sport education.* Champaign, IL: Human Kinetics.

Siedentop, D. (1998). What is sport education and how does it work? *Journal of Physical Education, Recreation, & Dance, 69*(4), 18-20.

Siedentop, D. & Tannehill, D. (2000). *Developing teaching skills in physical education* (4th ed.). Mountain View, CA: Mayfield.

Tannehill, D. (1998). Sport education introduction. *Journal of Physical Education, Recreation, & Dance, 69*(4), 16-17.

In the appendix you will find the following blank assessment documents: (a) a PASE activity task card; (b) a set of PASE fitness task cards; (c) a game performance assessment instrument (GPAI); and (d) a PASE roles and responsibilities checklist. These blank templates represent some of the more common assessment tools that are used in sport education. Teachers are encouraged to photocopy these documents and use them as they see fit. For suggestions on how to implement any of these tools please refer to the corresponding section of the text, which details the particular assessment strategy of interest. We hope that teachers experimenting with sport education find the appendix documents to be helpful as they strive to document, monitor, and enhance student learning in physical education.

PASE ACTIVITY TASK CARD

Skill:	Tactic:			

Learning Tasks		Self	Peer	Coach
E	1.			❑
E	2.	❑		
E	3.	❑		
E	4.	❑		
E	5.		❑	
A	6.	#___		❑
E	7.	❑		
E	8.	❑		
E	9.	❑		
E	10.		❑	
A	11.	#___		❑
E	12.	❑		
E	13.	❑		
E	14.	❑		
E	15.		❑	
A	16.	#___		❑
E	17.	❑		
A	18.	#___		❑
A	19.	#___		❑
A	20.	#___		❑

Key	E	Extension task	Series of tasks that progress from simple to complex.
	A	Application task	Self-testing or competitive tasks that provide an opportunity for students to practice using skills in a game-like situation.

PASE FITNESS TASK CARDS

Directions: With the help of the fitness trainer, select a warm-up card (A, B, or C) and complete as many of the activities (1-5) as possible during the team warm-up. Make sure to record each task that you complete to criteria on your personal fitness recording sheet.

A		Warm-Up Card	A
HR Component		Activity	Criteria
1	CVE		
2	MSE		
3	FLX		
4	MSE		
5	FLX		

B		Warm-Up Card	B
HR Component		Activity	Criteria
1	CVE		
2	MSE		
3	FLX		
4	MSE		
5	FLX		

C		Warm-Up Card	C
HR Component		Activity	Criteria
1	CVE		
2	MSE		
3	FLX		
4	MSE		
5	FLX		

GAME PERFORMANCE ASSESSMENT INSTRUMENT

Component	Criteria					
1.						
2.						
3.						

Team:						
	1.		2.		3.	
Name						

Key　　A = Appropriate　　　E = Efficient
　　　　　IA = Inappropriate　　IE = Inefficient

Components of Game Performance

Base	Appropriate return of performer to a "base" position between skill attempts
Decision Making	Making appropriate decisions about what to do with the ball (or projectile) during a game
Skill Execution	Efficient execution of selected skills
Support	Provides appropriate support for teammate with ball (or projectile) by being in position to receive a pass
Guard/Mark	Appropriate guarding/marking of an opponent who may or may not have the ball (or projectile)
Cover	Provides appropriate defensive cover, help, or backup for a player making a challenge for the ball (or projectile)
Adjust	Movement of performer, either offensively or defensively, as necessitated by the flow of the game

Name: _____

PASE ROLES AND RESPONSIBILITIES CHECKLIST

Directions: Use the shading to determine your role and corresponding responsibilities for the day's lesson. At the end of the lesson you will be asked to determine the responsibilities that you successfully completed. For each responsibility successfully completed, place a check [✔] in the box. For each responsibility that you did not successfully complete, place a [0] in the box. If you are the coach, then your role will not rotate and you will perform the coaching role for the entire season. All other roles will rotate on a regular basis as denoted by the shaded areas.

Roles and Responsibilities — Lesson

	1	2	3	4	5	6	7	8	9	10	11	12

Coach
- Leads skill and strategy practice
- Assists teacher when needed
- Makes decisions about team lineups
- Provides leadership for team

Fitness Trainer
- Selects appropriate warm-up activities
- Leads team warm-ups
- Reports injuries to teacher
- Aids teacher in administering first-aid

Statistician
- Records scores during contests
- Maintains ongoing team records
- Summarizes contest scores
- Provides final records to appropriate person

Official
- Manages contests
- Interprets rules during contests
- Mediates conflicts
- Maintains contest pacing

Sports Information Director
- Acquires compiled records from statistician
- Publicizes records via school newspaper, etc.
- Reports progress daily to teammates
- Assumes role responsibilities of absent teammates

Manager
- Inspects and cares for equipment
- Distributes equipment
- Monitors teammates' role performance
- Assumes administrative duties assigned by teacher
- Monitors time of lesson components
- Organizes home court space

RESOURCES

Published by the National Association for Sport and Physical Education for quality physical education programs:

Moving Into the Future: National Standards for Physical Education, A Guide to Content and Assessment (1995), Stock No. 304-10083

National Standards for Beginning Physical Education Teachers (1995), Stock No. 304-10085

Concepts of Physical Education: What Every Student Needs to Know (1998), Stock No. 304-10157

Sport and Physical Education Advocacy Kit (SPEAK) II (1999), Stock No. 304-10160

Physical Activity for Children: A Statement of Guidelines (1998), Stock No. 304-10175

Active Start: A Statement of Physical Activity Guidelines for Children Birth to Five Years (2002), Stock No. 304-10254

Appropriate Practice Documents

Appropriate Practice in Movement Programs for Young Children, (2000), Stock No. 304-10232

Appropriate Practices for Elementary School Physical Education (2000), Stock No. 304-10230

Appropriate Practices for Middle School Physical Education (2001), Stock No. 304-10248

Appropriate Practices for High School Physical Education (1998), Stock No. 304-10129

Opportunity to Learn Documents

Opportunity to Learn Standards for Elementary Physical Education (2000), Stock No. 304-10242

Physical Education Program Improvement and Self-Study Guides (1998) for Middle School, Stock No. 304-10173, for High School, Stock No. 304-10174

Assessment Series

Assessment in Outdoor Adventure Physical Education (2003), Stock No. 304-10218

Assessing Student Outcomes in Sport Education: A Pedagogical Approach (2003), Stock No. 304-10219

Video Tools for Teaching Motor Skill Assessment (2002), Stock No. 304-10217

Assessing Heart Rate in Physical Education (2002), Stock No. 304-10214

Authentic Assessment of Physical Activity for High School Students (2002), Stock No. 304-10216

Elementary Heart Health: Lessons and Assessment (2001), Stock No. 304-10215

Portfolio Assessment for K-12 Physical Education (2000), Stock No. 304-10213

Standards-Based Assessment of Student Learning: A Comprehensive Approach (1999), Stock No. 304-10206

Assessment in Games Teaching (1999), Stock No. 304-10212

Assessing Motor Skills in Elementary Physical Education (1999), Stock No. 304-10207

Assessing and Improving Fitness in Elementary Physical Education (1999), Stock No. 304-10208

Creating Rubrics for Physical Education (1999), Stock No. 304-10209

Assessing Student Responsibility and Teamwork (1999), Stock No. 304-10210

Preservice Professional Portfolio System (1999), Stock No. 304-10211

Order online at www.aahperd.org/naspe or call 1-800-321-0789

Shipping and handling additional.

National Association for Sport and Physical Education, an association of the American Alliance for Health, Physical Education, Recreation, and Dance

1900 Association Drive, Reston, VA 20191, naspe@aahperd.org, 703-476-3410